Galloway's Half Marathon Training

JEFF GALLOWAY

Galloway's Half Marathon Training

Use the Run Walk Run® Method to Finish Every Race Strong

Meyer & Meyer Sport

British Library Cataloguing in Publication Data

A catalogue record for this book is available from the British Library

Galloway's Half Marathon Training

Maidenhead: Meyer & Meyer Sport (UK) Ltd., 2021

ISBN: 978-1-78255-220-8

© 2006, 2021 by Meyer & Meyer Sport (UK) Ltd.
5th Edition of the 1st Edition 2006

Aachen, Auckland, Beirut, Dubai, Hägendorf, Hong Kong, Indianapolis, Cairo, Cape Town, Maidenhead, Manila, New Delhi, Singapore, Sydney, Tehran, Vienna

 Member of the World Sport Publishers' Association (WSPA), www.w-s-p-a.org

Printed by: Print Consult GmbH, Munich, Germany

Printed in Slovakia

ISBN: 978-1-78255-220-8
Email: info@m-m-sports.com
www.thesportspublisher.com

Contents

Chapter 1

WHY HAS THE HALF MARATHON BECOME SO POPULAR?

- Even after a difficult 13.1 mile (21K) race, runners can usually celebrate that evening

- Beginners who yearn to run a marathon see this distance as the first big step

- Marathoners find that the "half" keeps them in shape for their next "full"

- The distance is enough of a challenge to keep runners focused and energized

- Increasing long runs toward a half marathon race results in faster times at 5K, 10K, etc.

After studying findings of experts who specialize in ancient man, I've come to believe that training for long-distance events connects us directly to our roots. Primitive man had to walk and run for survival—thousands of miles a year. Through millions of years of evolution, the muscles, tendons, bones, energy systems and cardiovascular capacity adapted and expanded. A series of psychological rewards also developed, which make us feel good about ourselves when we run and walk at the correct pace in a consistent training program.

The primary goal of ancient migration was to reach the next destination. Likewise, the greatest joy for half marathoners comes in crossing the finish line. The perception among those who've run both marathons and half marathons is that running the "half" bestows more than half of the satisfaction and achievement of the "full".

There are quite a few lessons to be learned as one extends one's endurance limit beyond 13 miles or 21K: conservation of resources, pacing, fluid intake, blood sugar maintenance, etc. But making a mistake during "half" training does not incur the injury risk or the downtime experienced after marathon errors.

Veterans who've run the distance before will find in this book a series of highly successful training programs, based upon the time goal. You'll be introduced to other training components that will make the journey more interesting. Be careful if you're a veteran doing speed workouts: most of the injuries occur here. It is always best to be conservative.

If you find a way to enjoy a part of every run, your half marathon training can bring joy, satisfaction, achievement, and a positive sense of focus. For many, the challenge teaches individuals that they have unused hidden resources that can be used to deal with other challenges in life. Much of the success and joy comes from a unique endurance blending of body, mind and spirit.

Above all, you will find tools inside this book to take control over your fitness, your attitude, your endurance, your fatigue, your aches/pains, and your vitality. When you use these tools, you become the captain of an injury-free ship and can steer toward a number of positive experiences.

This book is written as one runner to another and is the result of more than 50 years of running, more than four decades of training for half and full marathons, and from having been the "coach" to more than 500,000 runners through my e-coaching, running schools, retreats, books, and individual consultations. None of the advice inside is offered as medical advice. To get help in this area, see a doctor or appropriate medical expert.

I salute all who put themselves to a realistic challenge. If you haven't done this before, you have one of life's great rewards waiting for you as you discover that you have much more strength inside than you envisioned.

Chapter 2

SETTING GOALS AND PRIORITIES

By focusing on a few key elements, you have the opportunity to take control over the enjoyment of the running experience. If you're preparing for your first 21K race, I recommend that you choose the "to finish" schedule, and run slower on every run than you could run on that day. Even after the 20th or 100th race, you're more likely to remember the details of your first one. Your mission, therefore, should be to weave the training runs, and the race itself, into a positive tapestry of memories that will enrich the rest of your life.

TOP 3 GOALS FOR FIRST TIME HALF MARATHON RUNNERS

1. Finish in the upright position,

2. with a smile on your face, and

3. wanting to do it again.

These three components define the first level of success in any training program, and the degree of enjoyment of each long run. If this is your first race experience at the 13.1 distance, visualize yourself coming across the finish line, demonstrating these three behaviors. The more you focus on this image, the more likely you are to realize this during most of your runs.

RUNNING ENJOYMENT

Find a way to enjoy parts of every run—even the speed training (if you are a time goal runner). Most of your runs should be....mostly enjoyable. You increase the pleasure of each run by inserting a few social/scenic/mentally refreshing runs every week. Your desire to take your next run, and move up your training to the half marathon and beyond, is enhanced by scheduling the fun sessions first, with one to three of them every week.

STAY INJURY FREE

When injured runners review their journal, they often find the causes of aches and pains. Make a list of past problems, and repeated challenges. After reading the injury section of this book, make the needed adjustments. As you eliminate the injury stress, you can eliminate most (or all) of your injuries.

AVOIDING OVERUSE OR BURNOUT

All of us get the warning signs of overtraining. Unfortunately, we often ignore these or don't know what they are. Your training journal is a wonderful tool for tracking any possible ache, pain, loss of desire, unusual fatigue that lingers, etc. If you develop an injury, you can review your journal and often find the reasons. This helps you to become more sensitive to future problems and make conservative adjustments in the plan to reduce upcoming injury risk.

BECOME THE CAPTAIN OF YOUR SHIP

When you balance stress and rest, running bestows a sense of satisfaction and achievement that is unsurpassed. Intuitively, we know that this is good for us, mentally and physically. When we decide to use the monitoring tools in this book we take a major amount of control over fatigue, injuries, energy level, and enjoyment of running.

WHEN TO SET A TIME GOAL

After finishing your first half marathon you may choose a time goal, after reading the "Predicting Race Performance" chapter. Many veterans (myself included) decide to stay within their capabilities, use the "to finish" schedule, and enjoy the experience.

I commend all who decide to take on an endurance challenge. Almost everyone who makes it to the finish line will tap into a mysterious and complex source of continuing strength and balance: the human spirit. Enjoy the journey!

Chapter 3

IMPORTANT HEALTH INFORMATION

MEDICAL CHECK

Check with your doctor's office before you start a strenuous training program. Keep the doctor informed of cardiovascular system irregularities or aches and pains that could be injuries. At first, just tell your physician or head nurse how much running you plan to be doing over the next year. Almost every person will be given the green light. If your doctor tells you not to run, ask why.

Since there are so few people who cannot train even for strenuous goals (if they use a liberal run walk run formula), I suggest that you get a second opinion if your doctor tells you not to run. Certainly the tiny number of people who should not run have good reasons. But the best medical advisor is one who wants you to get the type of physical activity that engages you—unless there are significant reasons not to do so.

RISKS: HEART DISEASE, LUNG INFECTIONS, SPEEDWORK INJURIES

Running tends to bestow a protective effect from cardiovascular disease. But more runners die of heart disease than any other cause, and are susceptible to the same risk factors as sedentary people. Like most other people, runners at risk usually don't realize it. I know of a number of runners who have suffered heart attacks and strokes who probably could have prevented them if they had taken a few simple tests. Some of these are listed below, but check with your doctor if you have any questions or concerns.

Your heart is the most important organ in your body. This short section is offered as a guide to help you take charge over your cardiovascular health to maintain a high level of fitness in the most important organ for longevity and quality of life. As always, you need to get advice about your individual situation from a cardiologist who knows you and specializes in this area.

Note: The information in this book is offered as advice from one runner to another, and is not meant to be medical advice. Having a doctor/advisor will not only help you through some problems more quickly, but contact with a responsive and supportive medical advisor will improve confidence and motivation, while reducing anxiety.

Risk Factors: Get checked IF you have two of these—or one that is serious

- Family history
- Family history of cardiovascular problems
- Poor lifestyle habits earlier in life (alcohol, drugs, poor diet, etc.)
- High fat/high cholesterol diet
- Have smoked—or still smoke
- Obese or severely overweight
- High blood pressure
- High cholesterol

Tests

- Stress test—heart is monitored during a run that gradually increases in difficulty.

- C-reactive protein—has been an indicator of increased risk.

- Heart scan—an electronic scan of the heart which shows calcification, and possible narrowing of arteries.

- Radioactive dye test—very effective in locating specific blockages. Talk to your doctor about this.

- Carotid ultrasound test—helps to tell if you're at risk for stroke.

- Ankle-brachial test—can detect plaque buildup in arteries throughout the body.

None of these are foolproof. But by working with your cardiologist, you can increase your chance of living until the muscles just won't propel you farther down the road—maybe beyond the age of 100.

SHOULD I RUN WHEN I HAVE A COLD?

There are so many individual health issues with a cold that you must talk with a doctor before you exercise when you have an infection.

Lung infection—don't run! A virus in the lungs can move into the heart and kill you. Lung infections are usually indicated by coughing.

Common cold? There are many infections that initially indicate a normal cold but are much more serious. At least call your doctor's office to get clearance before running. Be sure to explain how much you are running, and what, if any medication you are taking.

Infections of the throat and above the neck—most runners will be given the OK, but check with the doc.

RISK OF SPEED

There is an increased risk of both injuries and cardiovascular events during speed sessions. Be sure to get your doctor's OK before beginning a speed program. The advice inside this book is generally conservative, but when in doubt, take more rest, more days off, and run slower. In other words...be more conservative.

Chapter 4

PRACTICAL INFORMATION ON SHOES, EQUIPMENT, AND MORE

One of the wonderful aspects of running, in a complex world, is the simplicity of the experience. You can run from your house or office in most cases, using public streets or pedestrian walkways. Ordinary clothing works well most of the time and you don't need to join a country club or invest in expensive exercise equipment.

While running with another person can be motivating, most runners enjoy running alone on most of their runs. It helps, however, to have a "support team" as you go through the training (running companions, doctors, running shoe experts). You'll probably meet these folks through the running grapevine.

CONVENIENCE

If you have an option near home and office for each of the training components listed above, you will be more likely to do the workouts on your schedule—when you need to do them.

SHOES, THE PRIMARY INVESTMENT

Most runners decide, wisely, to spend a little time on the choice of a good running shoe. After all, shoes are the only real equipment needed. The shoe that is a good match for your feet can make running easier, while reducing blisters, foot fatigue and injuries.

Because there are so many different brands and models, shoe shopping can be confusing. The best advice....is to get the best advice. Going to a good running store, staffed by helpful and knowledgeable runners, can cut the time required and can usually lead you to a much better shoe choice than you would pick by yourself. For more information on this see *Galloway's Book on Running,* and the back section of this book.

BUY THE TRAINING SHOE FIRST

Go to the running store in your area with the most experienced staff. First you'll need a pair for long runs and easy running days. Veterans may want to get a racing shoe (or lightweight training shoe) later. Bring along your most worn pair of shoes (any shoes), and a pair of running shoes that has worked well for you. Wait until you are several weeks into your training before you decide to get a racing shoe if you feel you need one.

DO I NEED A RACING SHOE?

In most cases, racing shoes only speed you up by a few seconds a mile—but this may be what a veteran needs to reach a significant goal. After several weeks, if you feel that your training shoes are too heavy or "clunky", look at some lighter models. After you have broken them in, you can use the lighter shoes during speed sessions.

A WATCH

There are a lot of good, inexpensive watches which will give you accurate times during speed workouts and races. Any watch that has a stopwatch function will do the job. Be sure to ask the staff person in the store how to use the stopwatch function.

A few watches can make walk breaks easier by "beeping" after each running segment and then again after the walking segment. You can also invest in a Fitbit or other smartwatch.

CLOTHING: COMFORT ABOVE ALL

The "clothing thermometer" at the end of this book is a great guide. In the summer, you want to wear light, cool clothing. During cold weather, layering is the best strategy. You don't have to have the latest techno-garments to run. On most days an old pair of shorts and a T-shirt are fine. As you get into the various components of your plan, you will find outfits that make you feel better and motivate you to get in your run even on bad weather days. It is also OK to give yourself a fashionable outfit as a "reward" for running regularly for several weeks.

A TRAINING JOURNAL

The journal is such an important component in running that I have written a chapter about it. By using it to plan ahead and then later, to review your success and mistakes, you assume a major degree of control over your running future. You'll find it reinforcing to write down what you did each day, and miss that reinforcement when you skip. Be sure to read the training journal chapter, and you, too, can steer yourself more toward enjoyment and success.

WHERE TO RUN

It helps to have several different venues for the various workouts. Try to find two or more options for each:

Long runs—scenic, interesting areas are best—with some pavement and some softer surface if possible.

Pace work—a track or any accurately measured segment.

Races and tests—Look carefully at the course—avoid hills, too many turns, or even too much flat terrain if you usually train on rolling hills (in a non-hilly race, you will fatigue your flat running muscles more quickly, if you don't run long runs on flat terrain). Read the section on racing.

Drills—any safe running area with a secure surface.

SAFETY: TOP PRIORITY!

Pick a course that is away from car traffic, and is in a safe area—where crime is unlikely. Try to have two or more options for each of the components because variety can be very motivating.

SURFACE

With the correct amount of cushion, and the selection of the right shoes for you, pavement should not give extra shock to the legs or body. A smooth surface dirt or gravel path is best for most runners for the easy days. But beware of an uneven surface especially if you have weak ankles or foot problems. For your tests, speedwork, and drills, you may have to talk to your shoe experts to avoid blisters, etc. when running on certain types of surfaces. Watch the slant of the road, trail, track or sidewalk—flat is best.

PICKING A RUNNING COMPANION

On long runs and on easy days, don't run with someone who is faster than you—unless they are fully comfortable slowing down to an easy pace—that is...slow for you. It is motivating to run with someone who will go slow enough so that you can talk. Share stories, jokes, problems if you wish, and you'll bond together in a very positive way.

The friendships forged on runs can be the strongest and longest lasting—if you're not huffing and puffing (or puking) from trying to run at a pace that is too fast. On speed days, however, it sometimes helps to run with a faster person as long as you are running at the pace you should be running in each workout.

REWARDS

Rewards are important at all times. Be sensitive and provide reinforcements that will keep you motivated, and make the running experience a better one (more comfortable shoes, clothes, etc.).

Positive reinforcement works! Treating yourself to a smoothie after a hard run, taking a cool dip in a pool, going out to a special restaurant after a longer run—all of these can reinforce the successful completion of another week or month. Of particular benefit is having a snack, within 30 minutes of the finish of a run, that has about 200-300 calories, containing 80% carbohydrate and 20% protein. The products Accelerade and Endurox R4 are already formulated with this ratio for your convenience, and give you a recovery boost also.

AN APPOINTMENT ON THE CALENDAR

Write down each of your weekly runs, transposed from the schedule in this book, at least 1 week in advance, on your calendar or journal. Since each week is broken down for you in this book, you can use it as your guide. Sure, you can change if you have to. But by having a secure running slot, you will be able to plan for your run, and make it happen. Pretend that this is an appointment with your boss, or your most important client, etc. Actually, you are your most important client!

MOTIVATION TO GET OUT THE DOOR

There are three times when runners feel challenged to run: 1) early in the morning, 2) after work, or 3) before the tough workouts. In the motivation section there are rehearsals for challenging situations. You will find it much easier to be motivated once you experience a regular series of runs that make you feel good. When you run and walk at the right pace, with the right preparation, you feel better, can relate to others better, and have more energy to enjoy the rest of the day.

TREADMILLS ARE JUST AS GOOD AS STREETS FOR SHORT RUNS

More and more runners are using treadmills for at least 50% of their runs—particularly those who have small children. It is a fact that treadmills tend to tell you that you have gone farther or faster than you really have (but usually are not off by more than 10%). But if you run on a treadmill for the number of minutes assigned, at the effort level you are used to (no huffing and puffing), you will get close enough to the training effect you wish. To ensure that you have run enough miles, feel free to add 10% to your assigned mileage.

USUALLY NO NEED TO EAT BEFORE THE RUN

Most runners don't need to eat before runs that are less than 6 miles. The only exceptions are those with diabetes or severe blood sugar problems. Many runners feel better during a run when they have enjoyed a cup of coffee about an hour before the start. Caffeine engages the central nervous system, which gets all of the systems needed for exercise up and running to capacity, very quickly.

If your blood sugar is low, which often occurs in the afternoon, it helps to have a snack of about 100-200 calories, about 30 minutes before the run, that is composed of 80% carbohydrate and 20% protein. The Accelerade product has been very successful.

Chapter 5

THE GALLOWAY RUN WALK RUN METHOD

"Walk breaks let you control the amount of fatigue on your legs and body"

I doubt that you will find any training component that will help you in more ways than my Run Walk Run Method. I continue to be amazed, every week, at the reports of how these strategic walks help runners to enjoy the half marathon as they improve their finish time. When placed appropriately for the individual, walk breaks will erase fatigue, reduce stress, improve motivation, increase running enjoyment, speed up recovery, and allow the runner to finish with strength. Here's how it works.

WALK BEFORE YOU GET TIRED

Most of us, even when untrained, can walk for several miles before fatigue sets in, because walking is an activity that we can do efficiently for hours. Running is more work, because you have to lift your body off the ground and then absorb the shock of the landing, over and over.

The continuous use of the running muscles will produce more fatigue, aches, and pains than running at the same pace while taking walk breaks. If you walk before your running muscles start to get tired, you allow the muscle to recover instantly—increasing your capacity for exercise while reducing the chance of next-day soreness.

The "method" part involves having a strategy. By using a ratio of running and walking, you can manage your fatigue. Using this fatigue-reduction tool conserves resources and bestows mental confidence to cope with any challenges that can come later. Even when you don't need the extra strength and resiliency bestowed by the method, you will feel better during and after your run, and finish knowing that you could have gone farther.

"The run-walk-run method is very simple: you run for a short segment and then take a walk break, and keep repeating this pattern."

Walk breaks allow you to take control over fatigue, in advance, so that you can enjoy every run. By taking them early and often you can feel strong, even after a run that is very long for you. Beginners will alternate very short run segments with short walks. Even elite runners find that walk breaks on long runs allow them to recover faster. There is no need to be totally exhausted at the end of any long run.

WALK BREAKS....

- Give you control over the way you feel at the end.

- Erase fatigue.

- Push back your fatigue wall.

- Allow for endorphins to collect during each walk break—you feel good!

- Break up the distance into manageable units. ("two more minutes").

- Speed recovery.

- Reduce the chance of aches, pains and injury.

- Allow you to feel good afterward—carrying on the rest of your day without debilitating fatigue.

- Give you all of the endurance of the distance of each session—without the pain.

- Allow older runners or heavier runners to recover fast, and feel as good or better as during the younger (slimmer) days.

A SHORT AND GENTLE WALKING STRIDE

It's better to walk slowly, with a short stride. There has been some irritation of the shins, when runners or walkers maintain a stride that is too long. Relax and enjoy the walk.

NO NEED TO EVER ELIMINATE THE WALK BREAKS

Some beginners assume that they must work toward the day when they don't have to take any walk breaks at all. This is up to the individual, but is not recommended. Remember that you decide what ratio of run walk run to use. There is no rule that requires you to hold to any ratio on a given day. As you adjust the run-walk to how you feel, you gain control over your fatigue.

I've run for more than 50 years, and I enjoy running more than ever because of walk breaks. Each run I take energizes my day. I would not be able to run almost every day if I didn't insert the walk breaks early and often. I start most runs taking a short walk break after a minute of running. By 2 miles I am usually walking every 3-4 minutes. By 5 miles the ratio often goes to every 7-10 minutes. But there are days every year when I stay at 3 minutes and even a few days at 1 minute. On long runs, however, I set my ratio to be the most conservative I can imagine—and stay with it throughout.

HOW TO KEEP TRACK OF THE WALK BREAKS

There are several watches which can be set to beep when it's time to walk, and then beep again when it's time to start up again. Check our website (www.jeffgalloway.com) or a good running store for advice in this area.

RUN-WALK-RUN RATIOS

After having coached over 100,000 runners using walk breaks, I've come up with the following suggested ratios:

Pace per mile	Run amount	Walk amount
7:00	6 minutes	30 seconds
7:30	5 minutes	30 seconds
8:00	4 minutes	30 seconds (or 2/15)
8:30	3 minutes	30 seconds (or 2/20)
9:00	2 minutes	30 seconds
9:30-10:45	90 seconds	30 seconds (or 45/15 or 40/20)
10:45-12:15	1 minute	30 seconds (or 40/20 or 30/15)
12:15-14:30	15 seconds	30 seconds (or 20/20 or 15/15)
14:30-15:45	15 seconds	30 seconds
15:45-17:00	10 seconds	30 seconds
17:00-18:30	8 seconds	30 seconds (or 5/25)
18:30-20:00	5 seconds	30 seconds

Note: You may always divide each of the amounts by 2.
Example: instead of running 7 minutes/walking 30 seconds, you could run 3:30 and walk 15 seconds. This allows for you to walk through a water stop that is placed irregularly.

Chapter 6

CHOOSING THE RIGHT GOAL AND PACE

In this chapter you'll learn how to determine the right pace for you on long runs and in your half marathon race. Veterans will learn how much improvement can be expected, and whether they are on track for the goal at various times in the training program. As you approach your goal at the end of the program, you can use the "Galloway Performance Predictor" to determine what you will be capable of running in your race—and how to make adjustments for temperature.

PREDICTION STRATEGY: ONE-MILE TIME TRIAL (TT) OR TEST

About 1995 I started using a one-mile time trial (called a "magic mile") as a prediction tool. After working with hundreds and then thousands of runners, I've found that those who do three to four of these during a season can get a very realistic prediction of their current racing potential. By adding 2 min/mi to this time, runners will find an injury-reducing pace for the long runs—and a realistic pace for the race itself.

IN ORDER TO RUN THE TIME IN THE RACE INDICATED BY GALLOWAY'S PERFORMANCE PREDICTOR:

- You have done the training necessary for the goal—according to the training programs in this book

- You are not injured

- You run with an even-paced effort

- The weather on goal race day is not adverse (below 60°F or 14°C, no strong headwinds, no heavy rain or snow, etc.)

- There are no crowds to run through, or significant hills

THE "MAGIC MILE" TIME TRIAL

1. Go to a track, or other accurately measured course. One-mile is 4 laps around a track.

2. Warm up by walking for 5 minutes, then running 1 minute and walking 1 minute, then jogging an easy 800 meters (half mile or two laps around a track).

3. Do 4 acceleration-gliders. These are listed in the "Drills" chapter.

4. Walk for 3-4 minutes

5. Run fast—for you—for 4 laps. Use the walk break suggestions in this chapter, or run the way you want.

6. On your first time trial, don't run all-out from the start—ease into your pace after the first half (2 laps).

7. Warm down by reversing the warm-up.

8. A school track is the best venue. Don't use a treadmill because they tend to be notoriously uncalibrated, and often tell you that you ran farther or faster than you really did.

9. On each successive one, try to adjust pace in order to run a faster time.

10. Use the following formula to see what time is predicted in the goal races.

HOW HARD SHOULD I RUN THE TEST

During the first month of the program, run the magic mile once a week, in the middle of a Tuesday or Thursday run. The first one should be only slightly faster than you normally run. With each successive TT, pick up the pace and beat your time each week. By the fourth week, you should be running fairly close to your potential.

Run the first lap slightly slower than you think you can average. Take a short walk break as noted in the walk break suggestions in this chapter. If you aren't huffing and puffing you can pick up the pace a bit on the second lap. If you are huffing after the first lap, then just hold your pace on lap two—or reduce it slightly. Most runners benefit from taking a walk break after the second lap.

At the end of lap 3, the walk break is optional. It is OK to be breathing hard on the last lap. If you are slowing down on the last lap, start a little slower on the next test. When you finish, you should feel like you couldn't run more than about half a lap farther at that pace (if that). You may find that you don't need many walk breaks during the test—experiment and adjust.

GALLOWAY'S PERFORMANCE PREDICTOR

Step 1: Run your "magic mile" time trial (TT) (4 laps around the track).
Step 2: Compute your mile pace for the half marathon by multiplying by 1.2.

Example:

Mile time: 10:00
For half marathon pace, multiply 10 x 1.2 = 12 min/mi
For long run training pace, add 3 minutes per mile = 15 min/per mile

One-mile Time	(x 1.2) FAST Half Mar Pace	(add 2 min/mi) Long Run Training Pace
5:00	6:00	9:00
5:30	6:37	9:40
6:00	7:12	10:15
6:30	7:48	10:50
7:00	8:24	11:30
7:30	9:00	12:00
8:00	9:36	12:40
8:30	10:12	13:15
9:00	10:48	13:50
9:30	11:24	14:30
10:00	12:00	15:00
10:30	12:36	15:40
11:00	13:12	16:15
11:30	13:48	16:50
12:00	14:24	17:30
12:30	15:00	18:00
13:00	15:36	18:40
13:30	16:12	19:15
14:00	16:48	19:50
14:30	17:24	20:30
15:00	18:00	21:00
15:30	18:36	21:40
16:00	19:12	22:15

Note: The 1.2 multiplier assumes that you will be running about all-out effort by the end of the half marathon. Below 8 minutes, take a short break at the 800 or run continuously.

WALK BREAKS DURING THE ONE-MILE TIME TRIAL

Pace of the one-mile TT	# of seconds walking
8:00	5-10 sec every 2 laps
8:30	8-12 sec every 2 laps
9:00	10-15 sec every 2 laps
9:30	12-18 sec every 2 laps
10:00	5-8 sec every lap
10:30	7-10 sec every lap
11:00	9-12 sec every lap
11:30	10-15 sec every lap
12:00	11-16 sec every lap
12:30	12-17 sec every lap
13:00	13-18 sec every lap
13:30	14-19 sec every lap
14:00	15-20 sec every lap
14:30	16-21 sec every lap
15:00	17-22 sec every lap
15:30	18-23 sec every lap
16:00	19-24 sec every lap

FIRST-TIME HALF MARATHONERS: RUN TO FINISH ONLY

I strongly recommend that first-time half marathon runners should not attempt a time goal. Use the one-mile time trial to determine your long run pace (adding 3 minutes to the time multiplied by 1.2). During the race itself, I recommend running the first 10 miles at your training pace. During the last 3 miles you may run as you wish.

TIME GOAL RUNNERS MAY MAKE A "LEAP OF FAITH" GOAL PREDICTION

I have no problem allowing my e-coach athletes, who've run one or more half marathons, to choose a goal time that is faster than that predicted by the pre-test. As you do the speed training, the long runs and your test races, you should improve...but how much? In my experience this "leap of faith" should not exceed 3-5% improvement in a three-month training program.

1. Run the one-mile time trial.

2. Use the formula above to predict what you could run now, if you were trained for the half marathon.

3. Choose the amount of improvement during the training program (3-5%).

4. Subtract this from # 2—this is your goal time.

HOW MUCH OF A "LEAP OF FAITH"?

Over a 2-3 month training program		
Half marathon pre-test prediction	3% Improvement	5% Improvement
1:20 h	2:12 m	4:00 m
1:40 h	3:00 m	5:00 m
2:00 h	3:36 m	6:00 m
2:30 h	4:30 m	7:30 m
3:00 h	5:24 m	9:00 m

Half marathon finish time improvement		
Pre-test prediction	3%	5%
3:00 h	2:54:36 m	2:51:00 m
2:30 h	2:25:30 m	2:22:30 m
2:00 h	1:56:24 m	1:54:00 m

The key to goal setting is keeping your ego in check. From my experience, I have found that a 3% improvement is realistic. This means that if your half marathon time is predicted to be 3:00, then it is realistic to assume you could lower it by five and a half minutes if you do the speed training and the long runs as noted on my training schedules in this book. The maximum improvement, which is less likely, is a more aggressive 5% or 9 minutes off a three-hour half marathon.

In both of these situations, however, everything must come together to produce the predicted result. Even runners who shoot for a 3% improvement, do all the training as described, achieve their goal slightly more than 50% of the time during a racing season. The more aggressive performances usually result in success about 20% of the time. There are many factors that determine a time goal in a half marathon that are outside of your control: weather, terrain, infection, etc.

"MAGIC MILE" TIME TRIALS (TTS) GIVE YOU A REALITY CHECK

- Follow the same format as listed in the pre-test.

- By doing this as noted, you will learn how to pace yourself.

- Hint: it's better to start a bit more slowly than you think you can run.

- Walk breaks will be helpful for most runners. Read the section in this book for suggested ratios.

- Note whether you are speeding up or slowing down at the end, and adjust in the next TT.

- If you are not making progress then look for reasons and take action.

REASONS WHY YOU MAY NOT BE IMPROVING

1. You're overtrained and tired—if so, reduce your training, and/or take an extra rest day.

2. You may have chosen a goal that is too ambitious for your current ability.

3. You may have missed some of your workouts, or not been as regular with your training as needed.

4. The temperature may have been above 60°F (14°C). Above this, you will slow down (the longer the race, the bigger the effect heat will have on the result).

5. You ran the first lap or two too fast.

FINAL REALITY CHECK

Take the last four TTs, and eliminate the slowest time. Average the three remaining times to get a good prediction in your goal race. If the tests are predicting a time that is slower than the goal you've been training for, go with the time predicted by the "magic miles." It is strongly recommended that you run the first one-third of your goal race a few seconds per mile slower than the pace predicted by the TT average.

USE A JOURNAL!

Read the chapter on using a journal. Your chance of reaching your goal increases greatly when you use this very important instrument. Psychologically, you start taking responsibility for the fulfillment of your mission when you use a journal.

Note: During my competitive years, and the first decade I worked with other runners, I found a very beneficial prediction tool in *Computerized Running Training Programs* by Gerry Purdy and James Gardner. This book has been revised and re-published in print and software as *Running Trax*, by Track and Field News. This is a great resource and I highly recommend it.

Chapter 7

PRIMARY TRAINING COMPONENTS

Long runs—Run these very slowly—at least 3 min/mi slower than you could run in a half marathon as predicted by your one-mile TT. Insert the walk breaks that are suggested in the Run Walk Run chapter in this book—or take them more often than recommended. I have not found anyone who has run the long runs too slowly or has taken the walk breaks too often. Slower long runs build the same endurance as fast long runs—with little or no risk of injury or burnout.

Drills—Cadence Drills (CD) and Acceleration Gliders (Acg). These easy exercises teach your body to improve form, as you fine-tune you running mechanics. They are not exhausting—most runners say they energize an average run. Doing each of these drills, once a week, will improve speed and running efficiency.

Hills (h) build strength better than any other training component. Warm up by jogging slowly for a half mile. Then, do 4 acceleration-gliders (Acg). Start each hill at a jog, and pick up the turnover as you go over the top of the hill. Don't sprint, but you will be huffing and puffing. Shorten stride slightly as you go up the hill. See the section in this book on hill training.

Magic mile time trials (TT)—These are done every few weeks to monitor progress and overtraining.

- Go to a track, or other accurately measured course.

- Warm up by walking for 5 minutes, then running a minute and walking a minute, then jogging an easy 800 meters (half mile or two laps around a track).

- Do 4 acceleration-gliders. These are listed in the "Drills" chapter.

- Walk for 3-4 minutes.

- Run the one-mile TT—a hard effort. Follow the walk break suggestions.

- On your first TT, don't run all-out from the start—ease into your pace after the first third of the distance.

- Warm down by reversing the warm-up.

A school track is the best venue. Don't use a treadmill because they tend to be notoriously uncalibrated, and often tell you that you ran farther or faster than you really did. Run the first lap slightly slower than you think you can average. Take a short walk break as noted in the walk break suggestions in this chapter. It is OK to be huffing and puffing on the last lap. If you are slowing down on the last lap, start a little slower on the next test. When you finish, you should feel like you couldn't run more than about half a lap further at that pace (if that).

Speed (s)—A gradual increase in speed training can prepare you for the realistic goal of your choice. See the speedwork section of this book

Pace (p)—On these runs, you want to run at race pace, taking the walk breaks as you plan to take them in the race. This is like a dress rehearsal for race day. By doing this exactly as you plan to do in your race, you will be ready.

- Warm up with 5 min of walking, then 10 min of easy running and walking.

- Time yourself for a segment that is between half a mile and 1 mile.

- Run at your goal pace.

- Insert walk breaks as you plan to do in the race.

- Do 1-3 miles of these segments.

- Don't do them if your legs are too tired.

- Reverse the warm-up as a warm-down.

TRACK DISTANCES

400 meter—1 track lap (about a quarter mile)
800 meter—2 track laps (about a half mile)
1600 meter—4 track laps (about one mile)

These diverse elements are woven together throughout the training season so that you can continue to improve speed and endurance. The whole process is like a symphony of elements that blend mind and body, heart and legs, left brain and right into an integrated unit.

Chapter 8

BODY, MIND, AND SPIRIT RESPOND POSITIVELY TO TRAINING

THE "TEAM" OF HEART, LUNGS, NERVES, BRAIN, ETC.

Very often in college and professional sports, a group of very talented individuals is defeated by a solid team of players with lesser ability. In a similar way, running helps to mold your key body organs into a coordinated unit. When running within one's capacity, the right brain uses its intuitive and creative powers to solve problems, manage resources, and help us find the pace and amount of training that we can handle. While the heart is our primary blood pump, your leg muscles, when fit, will provide significant help in pushing blood back to the heart.

The heart gets stronger—like any muscle, the heart's strength and effectiveness is increased through regular endurance exercise.

The lungs—become more efficient in processing oxygen and inserting it into the blood.

Endorphins (natural painkillers)—reduce discomfort, and give you a relaxing and positive attitude.

THE LONG RUN BUILDS ENDURANCE

By gradually extending slow long runs, you train muscle cells to expand their capacity to utilize oxygen efficiently, sustain energy production, and in general, increase capacity to go farther. The continued increase in the distance of these long runs increases the reach of blood artery capillaries to deliver oxygen and improves the return of waste products so that the muscles can work at top capacity. In short, long runs bestow a better plumbing system, improving muscle capacity. These changes will pay off when you reach the end of your half marathon, and when you do speed training.

Even when running very slowly, with liberal walk breaks, you build endurance by gradually increasing the distance of a regularly scheduled long run. Start with the length of your current long one, and increase as noted in the following schedule:

MAINTAIN CURRENT ENDURANCE WITH TWO 30-MINUTE RUNS, EVERY OTHER DAY (I.E., TUESDAY AND THURSDAY)

A half hour run on Tuesday and Thursday will maintain the endurance gained on the weekend. This is the minimum and results in the lowest injury rate. If you are already running more than this, without aches and pains, you can continue if you wish—but be careful.

To summarize, the long runs on weekends, with two other runs during the week, will create a level of fitness and muscle strength sufficient to prepare for your goal in the half marathon. At the same time, you'll be improving the internal engineering of the muscles: enhanced oxygen absorption, increased blood flow, better energy supply and storage, and much more. Hills, speedwork and form drills improve the mechanical efficiency of the bones, muscles and tendons as they adapt, helping you to become a more efficient runner.

Chapter 9

HALF MARATHON TRAINING PROGRAMS

BEGINNER

This program is designed for those who have not been running regularly for a month or more. If you are already running more than 1 mile, look at the note below the training schedule.

1. What pace to run on the long runs? Read the chapter in this book on "Choosing the Right Goal...". After you run the one-mile TT (time trial), multiply by 1.2, then add 3 minutes—the result is your pace-per-mile on long runs at 60°F or cooler.

2. Run walk run ratio should correspond to the pace used, as noted in the run walk run chapter of this book.

3. Pace for the half marathon itself: Run the first 10 miles at the training pace, noted above. If you want speed up a little, you can do so during the last 3 miles.

4. On long runs and the race itself, slow down when the temperature rises above 60°F (14°C) by 30 sec a mile for every 5 degrees above 60°F or more (or by 20 sec/kilometer for every 2 degrees of temperature increase above 14°C).

5. Tuesday and Thursday runs can be done at the pace of your choice.

6. It is fine to do cross-training on Monday, Wednesday, and Friday if you wish. There will be little benefit to your running in doing this, but you'll increase your fat-burning capacity. Don't do exercises like stair machines that use the calf muscle.

7. Be sure to take a vacation from strenuous exercise, the day before your weekend runs.

	Mon	Tue	Wed	Thurs	Fri	Sat	Sun
1.	off	30 min run	off	30 min run	easy walk	off	1 mile
2.	off	30 min run	off	30 min run (TT)	easy walk	off	1.5 miles
3.	off	30 min run	off	30 min run (TT)	easy walk	off	2.0 miles
4.	off	30 min run	off	30 min run (TT)	easy walk	off	2.5 miles
5.	off	30 min run	off	30 min run (TT)	easy walk	off	3 miles
6.	off	30 min run	off	30 min run	easy walk	off	3.5 miles
7.	off	30 min run	off	30 min run	easy walk	off	4.0 miles
8.	off	30 min run	off	30 min run	easy walk	off	5K event
9.	off	30 min run	off	30 min run	easy walk	off	4.5 miles
10.	off	30 min run	off	30 min run	easy walk	off	5.0 miles
11.	off	30 min run	off	30 min run	easy walk	off	1 mile TT + 2 mi
12.	off	30 min run	off	30 min run	easy walk	off	5.5 miles
13.	off	30 min run	off	30 min run	easy walk	off	6.0 miles
14.	off	30 min run	off	30 min run	easy walk	off	3.0 miles
15.	off	30 min run	off	30 min run	easy walk	off	6.5 miles
16.	off	30 min run	off	30 min run	easy walk	off	1 mi TT + 2 mi

17. off	30 min run	off	30 min run	easy walk	off	7.0 miles
18. off	30 min run	off	30 min run	easy walk	off	7.5 miles
19. off	30 min run	off	30 min run	easy walk	off	3 miles
20. off	30 min run	off	30 min run	easy walk	off	8 miles
21. off	30 min run	off	30 min run	easy walk	off	8.5 miles
22. off	30 min run	off	30 min run	easy walk	off	1 mi TT
23. off	30 min run	off	30 min run	easy walk	off	9 miles
24. off	30 min run	off	30 min run	easy walk	off	3.0 miles
25. off	30 min run	off	30 min run	easy walk	off	10 miles
26. off	30 min run	off	30 min run	easy walk	off	4 miles
27. off	30 min run	off	30 min run	easy walk	off	11 miles
28. off	30 min run	off	30 min run	easy walk	off	1 mi TT + 3 mi
29. off	30 min run	off	30 min run	easy walk	off	12 miles
30. off	30 min run	off	30 min run	easy walk	off	4 miles
31. off	30 min run	off	30 min run	easy walk	off	13 miles
32. off	30 min run	off	30 min run	easy walk	off	1 mi TT + 3 mi
33. off	30 min run	off	30 min run	easy walk	off	14 miles
34. off	30 min run	off	30 min run	easy walk	off	4 miles
35. off	30 min run	off	30 min run	easy walk	off	Half marathon
36. off	30 min run	off	30 min run	easy walk	off	3-4 miles
37. off	30 min run	off	30 min run	easy walk	off	5-6 miles
38. off	30 min run	off	30 min run	easy walk	off	5-13 miles

Those who have run a long run within the last two weeks longer than one-mile can start on the week with a long run at your current long run distance. For example: If you ran 7 miles last weekend, you could start at week 17 or 18.

TO FINISH

1. This program is designed for those who have already been running regularly, but have never run a half marathon before, or for veterans who don't have a time goal. To begin this program, you should have a long run within the past two weeks of at least 7 miles. If your long run is not this long, then gradually increase the weekend run to this distance before beginning this program.

2. What pace to run on the long runs? Read the chapter in this book on "Choosing the Right Goal...". After you run the first one-mile TT (time trial), multiply by 1.2, then add 3 minutes—the result is your suggested long run pace per mile on long runs at 60°F or cooler.

3. Run walk run ratio should correspond to the pace used.

4. Pace for the half marathon itself: Run the first 10 miles at the training pace, noted above. If you want to speed up a little, you can do so at that point.

5. On long runs and the race itself, slow down when the temperature rises above 60°F by 30 sec a mile for every 5 degrees above 60°F or more.

6. Tuesday and Thursday runs can be done at the pace of your choice.

7. It is fine to do cross-training on Monday, Wednesday, and Friday if you wish. There will be little benefit to your running in doing this, but you'll increase your fat burning. Don't do exercises like stair machines that use the calf muscle.

8. Be sure to take a vacation from strenuous exercise the day before your weekend runs.

	Mon	Tue	Wed	Thurs	Fri	Sat	Sun
1.	off	30 min run	off	30 min run (TT)	easy walk	off	8 miles
2.	off	30 min run	off	30 min run	easy walk	off	1 mi TT + 3 mi
3.	off	30 min run	off	30 min run (TT)	easy walk	off	9 miles
4.	off	30 min run	off	30 min run (TT)	easy walk	off	4 miles
5.	off	30 min run	off	30 min run	easy walk	off	10 miles
6.	off	30 min run	off	30 min run	easy walk	off	1 mi TT + 4 mi
7.	off	30 min run	off	30 min run	easy walk	off	11 miles
8.	off	30 min run	off	30 min run	easy walk	off	5 miles
9.	off	30 min run	off	30 min run	easy walk	off	12 miles
10.	off	30 min run	off	30 min run	easy walk	off	1 mi TT + 4 mi
11.	off	30 min run	off	30 min run	easy walk	off	13 miles
12.	off	30 min run	off	30 min run	easy walk	off	5 miles
13.	off	30 min run	off	30 min run	easy walk	off	14 miles
14.	off	30 min run	off	30 min run	easy walk	off	1 mi TT + 4 mi
15.	off	30 min run	off	30 min run	easy walk	off	Half marathon
16.	off	30 min run	off	30 min run	easy walk	off	3-5 miles

TIME GOAL PROGRAM: 2:30-3:00

Note: This is the minimum that I've found necessary to prepare for the goal. If you are already running more than this amount, and are able to recover between workouts, you may continue to do what you are doing—but be careful.

1. To begin this program, you should have run a long run within the past two weeks of at least 7 miles. If your long run is not this long, then gradually increase the weekend run to this distance before starting this program.

2. What is my current level of performance? Read the chapter in this book on "Choosing the Right Goal...". After you run the first one-mile TT (time trial), multiply by 1.2. This tells you what you are currently capable of running in a half marathon right now, when the temperature is 60°F or below, and if you have done the long runs and speed training listed in the schedule.

3. What pace should I run on the long runs? Take your current performance level (one-mile TT x 1.2) and add 3 minutes—the result is your suggested long run pace per mile on long runs at 60°F or cooler.

4. Slow down when the temperature rises above 60°F by 30 sec a mile for every 5 degrees above 60°F.

5. Run walk run ratio should correspond to the pace used.

6. At the beginning of the program, after you have run the first one-mile TT, you can choose a goal that is as fast as 20 seconds per mile faster than predicted by the process indicated in # 2—or any goal slower than this. To use this schedule, the goal pace should be between 11:30 and 13:30.

7. To compute your pace for the 800-meter (2 laps around a track) repeats done on speedwork weekends, take half the time of your goal pace per mile, as you decided according to #6 above, and subtract 15 seconds.

8. Warm up for each 800-meter repeat workout by walking for 5 minutes, then jogging very slowly for 5-10 minutes. Then do 4-8 acceleration-gliders (see the segment about this in this book). Reverse this process as your warm-down, leaving out the acceleration gliders.

9. Walk 2:30 to 3 minutes between each 800-meter repeat.

10. At the end of the first lap, walk for 20-30 seconds—but don't stop your stopwatch. The time for each 800 should be from the start until the end of the second lap.

11. If you have recovered from the weekend workout on Tuesday, run a mile at race pace. After an easy warm-up, run 4 of the cadence drills (CD) and 4 acceleration-gliders (Acg). These are described in the drill section of this book. Then run a mile segment at goal pace, taking the walk breaks as you plan to do them in the race. Jog for the rest of your run.

12. On long runs and the race itself, slow down when the temperature rises above 60°F by 30 sec a mile for every 5 degrees above 60°F or more (20 sec/km for each 2°C above 14°C).

13. It is fine to do cross-training on Monday, Wednesday, and Friday if you wish. There will be little benefit to your running in doing this, but you'll increase your fat-burning potential. Don't do exercises like stair machines that use the calf muscle.

14. Be sure to take a vacation from strenuous exercise the day before your weekend runs.

15. On Thursday, run a few hill repeats (h), as described by the hill section in this book—except for the days set aside for the one-mile TTs.

	Mon	Tue	Wed	Thurs	Fri	Sat	Sun
1.	off	30 min run	off	30 min run (TT)	easy walk	off	8 miles
2.	off	30 min run	off	1 mi TT +1mi	easy walk	off	2 x 800m
3.	off	30 min run	off	30 min run (TT)	easy walk	off	9 miles
4.	off	30 min run	off	30 min run (TT)	easy walk	off	3 x 800m
5.	off	30 min run	off	30 min run	easy walk	off	10 miles
6.	off	30 min run	off	1 mi TT 1mi	easy walk	off	4 x 800m
7.	off	30 min run	off	30 min run	easy walk	off	11 miles
8.	off	30 min run	off	30 min run	easy walk	off	6 x 800m

(continued)

(continued)

9. off	30 min run	off	30 min run	easy walk	off	12 miles
10. off	30 min run	off	1 mi TT +1mi	easy walk	off	8 x 800m
11. off	30 min run	off	30 min run	easy walk	off	13.5 miles
12. off	30 min run	off	30 min run	easy walk	off	10 x 800m
13. off	30 min run	off	30 min run	easy walk	off	15 miles
14. off	30 min run	off	30 min run	easy walk	off	1 mi TT + 3 mi
15. off	30 min run	off	30 min run	easy walk	off	Half marathon
16. off	30 min run	off	30 min run	easy walk	off	3-5 miles

TIME GOAL PROGRAM: 1:59-2:29

Note: This is the minimum that I've found necessary to prepare for the goal. If you are already running more that this amount, and are able to recover between workouts, you may continue to do what you are doing—but be careful.

1. To begin this program, you should have run a long run within the past 2 weeks of at least 7 miles. If your long run is not this long, then gradually increase the weekend run to this distance. Read the "long run" section in this book.

2. What is my current level of fitness? Read the chapter in this book on "Choosing the Right Goal...". After you run the first one-mile TT (time trial), multiply by 1.2. This tells you what you are currently capable of running in a half marathon right now, when the temperature is 60°F or below and you have done the long runs and speed training listed in the schedule.

3. What pace should I run on the long runs? Take your current performance level (one-mile TT x 1.2) and add 3 minutes—the result is your suggested long run pace per mile on long runs at 60°F or cooler.

4. Slow down when the temperature rises above 60°F by 30 sec a mile for every 5 degrees above 60°F or more.

5.   Run walk run ratio should correspond to the pace used.

6.   At the beginning of the program, after you have run the first one-mile TT, you can choose a goal as fast as 20 seconds per mile faster than predicted by the process indicated in # 2—or any goal slower than this. To use this schedule, the goal pace should be between 11:30 and 9:20.

7.   To compute your pace for the 800-meter (2 laps around a track) repeats done on speedwork weekends, take half the time of your goal pace per mile, as you decided according to #6 above, and subtract 15 seconds.

8.   Warm up for each 800-meter repeat workout by walking for 5 minutes, then jogging very slowly for 5-10 minutes. Next, do 4-8 acceleration-gliders. Reverse this process as your warm-down, leaving out the acceleration gliders.

9.   Walk 2 minutes and run 30 seconds between each 800-meter repeat.

10. At the end of the first lap, walk for 15-25 seconds—but don't stop your stopwatch. The time for each 800 should be from the start until the end of the second lap.

11. If you have recovered from the weekend workout on Tuesday, run a mile at race pace. After an easy warm-up, run 4 of the cadence drills (CD) and 4 acceleration-gliders (acg). These are described in the drill section of this book. Then run a mile segment at goal pace, taking the walk breaks as you plan to do them in the race. Jog for the rest of your run.

12. On long runs and the race itself, slow down when the temperature rises above 60°F by 30 sec a mile for every 5 degrees above 60°F or more (20 sec/km for each 2°C above 14°C).

13. It is fine to do cross-training on Monday, Wednesday, and Friday if you wish. There will be little benefit to your running in doing this, but you'll increase your fat-burning potential. Don't do exercises like stair machines that use the calf muscle.

14. Be sure to take a vacation from strenuous exercise, the day before your weekend runs.

15. On Thursday, run a few hill repeats (h), as described by the hill section in this book—except for the days set aside for one-mile TTs.

	Mon	Tue (CD/ acg/p)	Wed	Thurs (hrs)	Fri	Sat	Sun
1.	off	30-45 min run	off	30-45min (TT)	easy walk	off	8 miles
2.	off	30-45 min run	off	1 mi TT +1mi	easy walk	off	3 x 800m
3.	off	30-45 min run	off	30-45min (TT)	easy walk	off	9.5 miles
4.	off	30-45 min run	off	30-45min (TT)	easy walk	off	5 x 800m
5.	off	30-45 min run	off	30-45 min run	easy walk	off	11 miles
6.	off	30-45 min run	off	1 mi TT 2mi	easy walk	off	7 x 800m
7.	off	30-45 min run	off	30-45 min run	easy walk	off	12.5 miles
8.	off	30-45 min run	off	30-45 min run	easy walk	off	9 x 800m
9.	off	30-45 min run	off	30-45 min run	easy walk	off	14 miles
10.	off	30-45 min run	off	1 mi TT +2mi	easy walk	off	11 x 800m
11.	off	30-45 min run	off	30-45 min run	easy walk	off	15 miles
12.	off	30-45 min run	off	30-45 min run	easy walk	off	12 x 800m
13.	off	30-45 min run	off	30-45 min run	easy walk	off	17 miles
14.	off	30-45 min run	off	30-45 min run	easy walk	off	13 x 800m
15.	off	30-45 min run	off	30-45 min run	easy walk	off	Half marathon
16.	off	30-45 min run	off	30-45 min run	easy walk	off	5 miles

TIME GOAL PROGRAM: 1:45-1:58

Note: This is the minimum that I've found necessary to prepare for the goal. If you are already running more that this amount, and are able to recover between workouts you may continue to do what you are doing—but be careful.

1.   To begin this program, you should have run a long run within the past two weeks of at least 7 miles. If your long run is not this long, then gradually increase the weekend run to this distance. Read the "long run" section in this book.

2.   What is my current level of fitness? Read the chapter in this book on "Choosing the Right Goal...". After you run the first one-mile TT (time trial), multiply by 1.2. This tells you what you are currently capable of running in a half marathon right now, when the temperature is 60°F or below and you have done the long runs and speed training listed in the schedule.

3.   What pace should I run on the long runs? Take your current performance level (one-mile TT x 1.2) and add 2 minutes and 30 seconds—the result is your suggested long run pace per mile on long runs at 60°F or cooler.

4.   Slow down when the temperature rises above 60°F by 30 sec a mile for every 5 degrees above 60°F or more (20 sec/km for each 2°C above 14°C).

5.   Run walk run ratio should correspond to the pace used, as noted in the run walk run chapter of this book.

6.   At the beginning after running the first one-mile TT, you can choose a goal as fast as 20 seconds per mile faster than predicted by the process indicated in # 2—or any goal slower than this. To use this schedule, the goal pace should be between 8:00 and 9:19.

7.   To compute your pace for the 800-meter repeats done on speedwork weekends, take half the time of your goal pace per mile, as you decided according to #6 above, and subtract 15 seconds.

8.   Warm up for each 800-meter repeat workout by walking for 5 minutes, then jogging very slowly for 5-10 minutes. Reverse this process as your warm-down.

9.   Walk 2 min between each 800-meter repeat.

10. At the end of the first lap, walk for 15-20 seconds without stopping your stopwatch. Many runners find that they recover faster from the long workouts when they do this. The time for each 800 should be from the start until the end of the second lap.

11. If you have recovered from the weekend workout on Tuesday, run a mile at race pace (noted as "p" on the Tue line). After an easy warm-up, run 4 of the cadence drills (CD) and acceleration-gliders (acg). These are described in the drill section of this book. Then run a mile segment at goal pace, taking the walk breaks as you plan to do them in the race. Jog for the rest of your run.

12. On long runs and the race itself, slow down when the temperature rises above 60°F by 30 sec a mile for every 5 degrees above 60°F or more (20 sec/km for each 2°C above 14°C).

13. It is fine to do cross-training on Monday, Wednesday, and Friday if you wish. There will be little benefit to your running in doing this, but you'll increase your fat-burning potential. Don't do exercises like stair machines that use the calf muscle.

14. Be sure to take a vacation from strenuous exercise the day before your weekend runs.

15. On Thursday, run a few hill repeats (h), as described by the hill section in this book—except for the days set aside for one-mile TTs.

	Mon	Tue (CD/ acg/p)	Wed	Thurs (hrs)	Fri	Sat	Sun
1.	off	40-60 min run	off	40-60min (TT)	25 min	off	8 miles
2.	off	40-60 min run	off	1 mi TT +3mi	25 min	off	5 x 800m
3.	off	40-60 min run	off	40-60min (TT)	25 min	off	9.5 miles
4.	off	40-60 min run	off	40-60min (TT)	25 min	off	7 x 800m
5.	off	40-60 min run	off	40-60 min run	25 min	off	11 miles
6.	off	40-60 min run	off	1 mi TT +4mi	25 min	off	9 x 800m
7.	off	40-60 min run	off	40-60 min run	25 min	off	12.5 miles
8.	off	40-60 min run	off	40-60 min run	25 min	off	11 x 800m

9.	off	40-60 min run	off	40-60 min run	25 min	off	14 miles
10.	off	40-60 min run	off	1 mi TT +4mi	25 min	off	12 x 800m
11.	off	40-60 min run	off	40-60 min run	25 min	off	16 miles
12.	off	40-60 min run	off	40-60 min run	25 min	off	13x 800m
13.	off	40-60 min run	off	40-60 min run	25 min	off	19 miles
14.	off	40-60 min run	off	40-60 min run	25 min	off	14 x 800m
15.	off	30-45 min run	off	30-45 min run	20 min	off	Half marathon
16.	off	30-45 min run	off	30-45 min run	20 min	off	5 miles

TIME GOAL PROGRAM: 1:30-1:44

Note: This is the minimum that I've found necessary to prepare for the goal. If you are already running more that this amount, and are able to recover between workouts, you may continue to do what you are doing—but be careful.

1. To begin this program, you should have run a long run within the past two weeks of at least 7 miles. If your long run is not this long, then gradually increase the weekend run to this distance. Read the "long run" section in this book.

2. What is my current level of fitness? Read the chapter in this book on "Choosing the Right Goal...". After you run the first one-mile TT (time trial), multiply by 1.2. This tells you what you are currently capable of running in a half marathon right now, when the temperature is 60°F or below and you have done the long runs and speed training listed in the schedule.

3. What pace should I run on the long runs? Take your current performance level (one-mile TT x 1.2) and add 2 minutes and 30 seconds—the result is your suggested long run pace per mile on long runs at 60°F or cooler.

4. Slow down when the temperature rises above 60°F by 30 sec a mile for every 5 degrees above 60°F or more (20 sec/km for each 2°C above 14°C).

5. Run walk run ratio should correspond to the pace used.

6. At the beginning of the program, after you have run 2-3 one-mile TTs, you can choose a goal as fast as 20 seconds per mile faster than predicted by the process indicated in # 2—or any goal slower than this. To use this schedule, the goal pace should be between 8:00 and 6:50.

7. To compute your pace for the 800-meter (2 laps around a track) repeats done on speedwork weekends, take half the time of your goal pace per mile, as you decided according to #6 above, and subtract 15 seconds.

8. Warm up for each 800-meter repeat workout by walking for 5 minutes, then jogging very slowly for 5-10 minutes. Reverse this process as your warm-down.

9. Walk 2 min between each 800-meter repeat.

10. At the end of the first lap, walk for 10-15 seconds, if you wish—but don't stop your stopwatch. Many runners find that they recover faster when they do this. The time for each 800 should be from the start until the end of the second lap.

11. If you have recovered from the weekend workout on Tuesday, run a mile at race pace (noted as "p" on the Tue line). After an easy warm-up, run 4 of the cadence drills (CD) and acceleration-gliders (acg). These are described in the drill section of this book. Then run a mile segment at goal pace, taking the walk breaks as you plan to do them in the race. Jog for the rest of your run.

12. On long runs and the race itself, slow down when the temperature rises above 60°F by 30 sec a mile for every 5 degrees above 60°F or more (20 sec/km for each 2°C above 14°C).

13. It is fine to do cross-training on Monday, Wednesday, and Friday if you wish. There will be little benefit to your running in doing this, but you'll increase your fat-burning potential. Don't do exercises like stair machines that use the calf muscle.

14. Be sure to take a vacation from strenuous exercise the day before your weekend runs.

15. On Thursday, run a few hill repeats (h), as described by the hill section in this book—except for the one-mile TTs.

Mon	Tue (CD/ acg/p)	Wed	Thurs (hrs)	Fri	Sat	Sun
1. off	40-60 min run	off	40-60min (TT)	25 min	off	8 miles
2. off	40-60 min run	off	1 mi TT +3mi	25 min	off	5 x 800m
3. off	40-60 min run	off	40-60min (TT)	25 min	off	9.5 miles
4. off	40-60 min run	off	40-60min (TT)	25 min	off	7 x 800m
5. off	40-60 min run	off	40-60 min run	25 min	off	11 miles
6. off	40-60 min run	off	1 mi TT +4mi	25 min	off	9 x 800m
7. off	40-60 min run	off	40-60 min run	25 min	off	13 miles
8. off	40-60 min run	off	40-60 min run	25 min	off	11 x 800m
9. off	40-60 min run	off	40-60 min run	25 min	off	15 miles
10. off	40-60 min run	off	1 mi TT +4mi	25 min	off	12 x 800m
11. off	40-60 min run	off	40-60 min run	25 min	off	17 miles
12. off	40-60 min run	off	40-60 min run	25 min	off	13 x 800m
13. off	40-60 min run	off	40-60 min run	25 min	off	19 miles
14. off	40-60 min run	off	40-60 min run	25 min	off	14 x 800m
15. off	30-45 min run	off	30-45 min run	20 min	off	Half marathon
16. off	30-45 min run	off	30-45 min run	20 min	off	5 miles

TIME GOAL PROGRAM: 1:15-1:29

Note: This is the minimum that I've found necessary to prepare for the goal. If you are already running more that this amount, and are able to recover between workouts, you may continue to do what you are doing—but be careful.

1. To begin this program, you should have run a long run within the past two weeks of at least 7 miles. If your long run is not this long, then gradually increase the weekend run to this distance. Read the "long run" section in this book.

2. What is my current level of fitness? Read the chapter in this book on "Choosing the Right Goal...". After you run the first one-mile TT (time trial), multiply by 1.2. This tells you what you are currently capable of running in a half marathon right now, when the temperature is 60°F or below and you have done the long runs and speed training listed in the schedule.

3. What pace should I run on the long runs? Take your current performance level (one-mile TT x 1.2) and add 2 minutes and 30 seconds—the result is your suggested long run pace per mile on long runs at 60°F or cooler.

4. Slow down when the temperature rises above 60°F by 30 sec a mile for every 5 degrees above 60°F or more (20 sec/km for each 2°C above 14°C).

5. Run walk run ratio should correspond to the pace used.

6. At the beginning of the program, after you have run 2-3 one-mile TTs, you can choose a goal as fast as 20 seconds per mile faster than predicted by the process indicated in # 2—or any goal slower than this. To use this schedule, the goal pace should be between 5:30 and 6:50.

7. To compute your pace for the 800-meter (2 laps around a track) repeats done on speedwork weekends, take half the time of your goal pace per mile, as you decided according to #6 above, and subtract 15 seconds.

8. Warm up for each 800-meter repeat workout by walking for 5 minutes, then jogging very slowly for 5-10 minutes. Reverse this process as your warm-down.

9. Walk 1:30 to 2 minutes between each 800-meter repeat.

10. At the end of the first lap, walk for 5-10 seconds, if you wish—but don't stop your stopwatch. Many runners find that they recover faster from the longer workouts by doing this. The time for each 800 should be from the start until the end of the second lap.

11. If you have recovered from the weekend workout on Tuesday, run a mile at race pace. After an easy warm-up, run 4 of the cadence drills (CD) and acceleration-gliders (acg). These are described in the drill section of this book. Then run a mile segment at goal pace, taking the walk breaks as you plan to do them in the race. Jog for the rest of your run.

12. On long runs and the race itself, slow down when the temperature rises above 60°F by 30 sec a mile for every 5 degrees above 60°F or more (20 sec/km for each 2°C above 14°C).

13. It is fine to do cross-training on Monday, Wednesday, and Friday if you wish. There will be little benefit to your running in doing this, but you'll increase your fat-burning potential. Don't do exercises like stair machines that use the calf muscle.

14. Be sure to take a vacation from strenuous exercise the day before your weekend runs.

15. On Thursday, run a few hill repeats (h), as described in the hill section in this book—except on the days when time trials are scheduled.

GALLOWAY'S HALF MARATHON TRAINING

	Mon	Tue (CD/acg/p)	Wed	Thurs (hrs)	Fri	Sat	Sun
1.	off	40-60 min run	off	40-60min (TT)	25 min	off	8 miles
2.	off	40-60 min run	off	1 mi TT +3mi	25 min	off	5 x 800m
3.	off	40-60 min run	off	40-60min (TT)	25 min	off	10 miles
4.	off	40-60 min run	off	40-60 min run	25 min	off	7 x 800m
5.	off	40-60 min run	off	40-60 min run	25 min	off	12 miles
6.	off	40-60 min run	off	1 mi TT +4mi	25 min	off	9 x 800m
7.	off	40-60 min run	off	40-60 min run	25 min	off	14 miles
8.	off	40-60 min run	off	40-60 min run	25 min	off	11 x 800m
9.	off	40-60 min run	off	40-60 min run	25 min	off	16 miles
10.	off	40-60 min run	off	1 mi TT +4mi	25 min	off	12 x 800m
11.	off	40-60 min run	off	40-60 min run	25 min	off	18 miles
12.	off	40-60 min run	off	40-60 min run	25 min	off	13 x 800m
13.	off	40-60 min run	off	40-60 min run	25 min	off	20 miles
14.	off	40-60 min run	off	40-60 min run	25 min	off	14 x 800m
15.	off	30-45 min run	off	30-45 min run	20 min	off	Half marathon
16.	off	30-45 min run	off	30-45 min run	20 min	off	5 miles

Chapter 10

THE DRILLS TO MAKE RUNNING FASTER AND EASIER

The following drills have helped thousands of runners run more efficiently and faster. Each targets a few key capabilities. When you put all of them together, they can help you run lighter on your feet, with better form, while strengthening key muscle groups. When runners do these regularly, I've seen them eliminate excess motion of feet and legs, reduce impact, reduce the effort of running, and increase the cadence or turnover of feet and legs. Each drill teaches you to run more directly and efficiently.

WHEN?

These should be done on a non-long-run day. It is fine, however, to do them as part of your warm-up, before a race or a speed workout. Many runners have also told me that the drills are a nice way to break up an average run they sometimes call "boring".

CADENCE OR TURNOVER DRILL (CD)

This is an easy drill that improves the efficiency of running, making running easier. This drill helps to pull all the elements of good running form together at the same time. Over the weeks and months, if you do this drill once every week, you will find that your normal cadence slowly and naturally increases.

1. Warm up by walking for 5 minutes, and running and walking very gently for 10 minutes.

2. Start jogging slowly for 1-2 minutes, and then time yourself for 30 seconds. During this half-minute, count the number of times your left foot touches the ground.

3. Walk around for a minute or so.

4. On the second 30-second drill, increase the count by 1 or 2.

5. Repeat this 3-7 more times, each time trying to increase by 1-2 additional counts.

6. If you reach a count that you can't exceed, just try to maintain.

In the process of improving turnover, the body's internal monitoring system coordinates a series of adaptations which helps the feet, legs, nervous system, and timing mechanism work together as an efficient team.

- Your foot touches more gently.

- Extra, inefficient motions of the foot and leg are reduced or eliminated.

- Less effort is spent on pushing up or moving forward.

- You stay lower to the ground.

- The ankle becomes more efficient.

- Ache and pain areas are not overused.

ACCELERATION-GLIDER DRILLS (ACG)

This drill is a form of speed play, or fartlek. By using it regularly, you develop a range of speeds, with the muscle conditioning to move smoothly from one to the next. The greatest benefit comes as you learn how to "glide", or coast off your momentum.

HERE'S HOW IT'S DONE

- Start by jogging very slowly for about 15 steps.

- Then, jog faster for about 15 steps—increasing to a regular running pace for you.

- Now, over the next 15 steps, gradually increase the speed to your current race pace.

- OK, it's time to glide, or coast. Allow yourself to gradually slow down to a jog using momentum as long as you can. At first you may only glide for 4 or 5 steps. As the months go by you will get up to 20, then 30 and beyond....you're gliding!

KEEP IN MIND

1. Acg drills are done on a non-long-run day, in the middle of a shorter run, or as a warm-up for a speed session or a race—or test day.

2. Warm up with at least half a mile of easy running.

3. Many runners do the turnover drill just after the easy warm-up, and then do the acceleration-gliders. But these can be done separately from the turnover drill, if desired.

4. Run 4-8 of them.

5. Do this at least once a week.

6. No sprinting—never run all-out.

After teaching this drill at my one-day running schools and weekend retreats for years, I can say that most people learn better through practice when they work on the concepts listed below—rather than the details—of the drill. So just get out there and try them!

Gliding—The most important concept. This is like coasting off the momentum of a downhill run. You can do some of your gliders running down a hill if you want, but it is important to do at least two of them on the flat land. Your goal is to use your momentum, if only for 5-10 strides, gliding for as many steps as you can.

Do this every week—As with the turnover drills, the regularity of the drill is very important. If you're like most runners, you won't glide very far at first. Regular practice will help you glide farther and farther.

Don't sweat the small stuff—I've included a general guideline of how many steps to do with each part of the drill, but don't worry about getting an exact number of steps. It's best to get into a flow with this drill and not worry about how many steps you are taking.

Smooth transition—between each of the components. Each time you "shift gears" you are using the momentum of the current mode to move you into the next mode. Don't make a sudden and abrupt change, but strive for a smooth transition between modes.

Overall purpose— As you do this drill, every week, you will feel smoother at each mode of running. Congratulations! You are learning how to keep moving at a fairly fast pace without using much energy. This is the main object of the drill.

There will be some weeks when you will glide longer than others—don't worry about this. By doing this drill regularly, you will find yourself coasting or gliding down the smallest of inclines, and even for 10-20 yards on the flat, on a regular basis. Gliding conserves energy, reduces fatigue, and can help you maintain faster pace in races.

Chapter 11

HILL TRAINING BUILDS STRENGTH AND MORE

Hill training strengthens the legs for running better than any other activity I know. At the same time it can help you maximize your stride length, increase leg speed, and improve your ability to run hills in races. The hill training segments provide a gentle introduction to faster running, while improving your capacity to perform speedwork later in the program.

Beginners shouldn't do hill training. If you've run several road races, you could run one to four hills (as mentioned below) on one of the short runs during the week. More experienced runners can follow the scheduled hill sessions in the schedules in this book.

THE HILL WORKOUT

- Walk for 5 minutes.

- Warm-up: Jog and walk to a hill—about 10 minutes. Jog a minute and walk a minute (a longer warm-up is fine).

- Do 4 acceleration-gliders. These are listed in the "Drills" chapter (don't sprint).

- Reverse the warm-up as your warm-down.

- Choose a hill with a gentle grade—steep hills often cause problems and bestow no benefit.

- Walk to the top of the hill. Then step off the length of your hill segment by walking down from the top:

    - 50 walking steps for those new to hill training

    - 100-150 steps for those who have done very little speed work before

    - 150-200 steps for those who have done speedwork, but not within the past six months

    - 200-300 steps for those who have been doing regular speedwork

- Mark the place after you count the steps. This is where each hill starts.

- Run up the hill for 5 seconds, and then down for 5 seconds.

- Walk for 30-60 seconds. Repeat this 5-10 times. This finalizes the warm-up.

- Walk for 3-4 minutes.

- Run the first few steps of each hill acceleration at a jog, then gradually pick up the turnover of the feet as you go up the hill.

- Get into a comfortable rhythm, so that you can gradually increase this rhythm or turnover (# of RPMs of feet and legs) as you go up the hill.

- Run with a relaxed stride—and keep shortening stride as you go up the hill.

- It's OK to huff and puff at the top of the hill—but don't let the legs get overextended, or feel exhausted.

- Run over the top of the hill by at least 10 steps.

- Jog back to the top of the hill and walk down to recover between each hill. Walk as much as you need for complete recovery after each hill.

HILL RUNNING FORM

- Start with a comfortable stride—fairly short.

- As you go up the hill, shorten the stride.

- Touch lightly with your feet.

- Maintain a body posture that is perpendicular to the horizon (upright, not leaning forward or back).

- Pick up the turnover of your feet as you go up and over the top.

- Keep adjusting stride so that the leg muscles don't tighten up—you want them as resilient as possible.

- Walk more if needed before running the next hill.

HILL TRAINING STRENGTHENS LOWER LEGS AND IMPROVES RUNNING FORM

The incline of the hill forces your legs to work harder as you go up. The extra work up the incline and the faster turnover builds strength. By taking an easy walk between the hills, and an easy day afterward, the lower leg muscles recover and rebuild, becoming stronger. Over several months, the improved strength allows you to go farther while supporting your body weight on your feet. An extended range of motion of the ankle and Achilles tendon results in a "bonus" extension of the foot—with no increase in effort. You will run faster without working harder. What a deal!

RUNNING FASTER ON HILLS IN RACES

Once you train yourself to run with efficient hill form, you'll run faster with increased turnover on the hill workouts. This prepares you to do the same in races. You won't run quite as fast in a race as in your workouts. But through hill training you can run faster than you used to run up the same hill on a race course.

Race hill technique is the same as in workouts: keep shortening your stride as you move up the hill. Monitor your respiration rate: don't huff and puff more than you were doing on the flat. As runners improve their hill technique in races, they find that a shorter and quicker stride reduces effort while increasing speed—with no increase in breathing.

Note: On your long runs and easy running days, just jog up hills, don't run faster up the hill. If your breathing is increasing on a hill, reduce effort and stride length until your respiration is as it was on the flat ground.

DOWNHILL FORM

- Run light on your feet.
- Maintain an average stride—avoid the temptation to extend the stride.
- Keep feet low to the ground.
- Let gravity pull you down the hill.
- Turnover of the feet will pick up.
- Try to glide (or coast) quickly down the hill.
- You shouldn't have to use your quad muscles (front of thigh) once you use this technique.

BIGGEST MISTAKES: TOO LONG A STRIDE, BOUNCING TOO MUCH

Even when your stride length is one or two inches too long, your downhill speed can get out of control. If you are bouncing more than an inch or two off the ground you run the risk of pounding your feet, having to use your quads to slow down (producing soreness) and creating hamstring soreness due to overstride. Best indicator of overstriding is having tight hamstrings (the big muscle behind your upper leg).

Chapter 12

SPEED TRAINING PREPARES YOU FOR TOP PERFORMANCE

At some point, virtually every runner wants to run a little faster. Often this is due to the envy of others who started when you did, but have recorded faster finish times a year later. Beware! Some very sedentary people inherited a better set of fitness genes. The reality is that the first item most runners desire, when they want to add spice to their running, is a faster pace. This chapter will explain how speed training helps, and the internal changes that allow you to run faster.

I don't recommend training for a time goal in your first half marathon. After you've finished your first campaign, come back to this chapter. During your first 21K training program, focus on the sense of satisfaction and achievement from continuing to push back your endurance through the long runs. Success is *finishing*.

Learn your limits. Most people go through their lives without ever testing their physical limits or experiencing the enriching experience of extending them. Once into this process, some get swept away in the quest for improvement. When runners make speed-training mistakes, they usually do too much, too soon. The series of gentle increases in the training schedules in this book will gradually extend your capacity to go farther—at a slightly faster pace than you are running now. Since each person can control the effort level, you will have a chance to limit the damage. The testing process involves guessing and adjusting, going just a bit farther and then backing off. When done regularly, speed-training prepares mind, body, and spirit for greater challenges.

Each workout will provide a slight increase in the number of speed repetitions. At the same time you improve your muscle conditioning and cardiovascular performance, you'll gain pace judgement and mental toughness. The overall experience of doing this, even for one season, progressively reduces race day anxiety as it develops confidence in confronting challenges in other areas of life. The only way I've found to prepare for pushing beyond the point of fatigue in races is to simulate the conditions during speed workouts.

Beware of the ego. Some of the most timid beginning runners become overly aggressive competitors. As you find your times improving through regular training, the ego tells you what you want to hear. "If you improved 10 seconds with one weekly speed workout, then two hard workouts will double the improvement." Many runners have allowed their egos to mistakenly focus the satisfaction from a run only on the finish time.

This can reduce the wonderful enjoyment of a gentle run. An ego-driven runner loses the glow of endorphins when the watch tells them that they didn't run as fast as he/ she should. This line   of thinking often leads to slower races (due to overtraining) and disappointment. Even when times are improving, if time improvement is your primary reward from running, you'll often miss the enjoyment of an achievement on the way to the next time goal. My suggestion: take time to enjoy the best part of the run: the vitality and mental attitude boost.

It is healthy to let your ego have its moments of glory as you perform well. Just realize that improvement is not continually an upward curve, and the ego has a problem with any downturn. A natural selection process occurs during a speed-training season, as the ego is forced to deal with reality, and make adjustments. But by maintaining the enjoyment of a fun run every week, and appreciating the afterglow from any run, you can maintain a balanced set of rewards, while keeping the ego in check.

While testing yourself for faster times can keep you focused, and may increase motivation, the blending of mind, body and spirit is maintained primarily through the enjoyment of the act of running. I've found that this is best done on slow runs, and in the slow warm-up and warm-down jogs that bracket your workouts. I've experienced an almost continuous stream of enjoyment from running for more than half a century.

It keeps getting better because I have regular doses of relaxing runs. Even when I was training for the Olympics, about 90% of my weekly miles were spent running at a slow and enjoyable pace.

Performance increase is not a continuous upward trek. Be prepared to record times on at least half of your tests that are slower than you think you should be running. This is often due to the ego telling you to run faster than your current ability. Be patient, learn from your setbacks, and you will generally move forward.

So take the leap of faith, and jump into the speed improvement process. By pushing the limits you may learn more about yourself than in any other activity in life. The real treasure is ahead: finding hidden strengths that help you get though even the toughest of tests —in races and in life itself.

GETTING FASTER REQUIRES EXTRA WORK

To get faster, you must push beyond your current performance capacity. But you must be careful. Even a small amount over your speed limit can result in longer recovery or injury. The secret is to run only a little harder on each workout, then back off so the systems can rebound and improve. Gradual and gentle increases are always better because you are more likely to sustain continuous and long-term improvement.

Our bodies are programmed to conserve resources by doing the smallest amount of work they can get away with. So even after we have increased the length of our runs steadily over several months, our leg muscles, tendons, ligaments etc. are not prepared for the jolt that speed-training delivers. The best way to stay injury free is to gradually increase the duration and intensity. But only when we put the legs, the heart, the lungs, etc. to a gentle test, week by week, does the body respond by improving in dozens of ways:

- Mitochondria (energy powerhouses inside muscle cell) increase capacity and output.

- Mechanical efficiency of the foot is improved—more work done with less effort.

- Legs go farther when tired—adaptations allow you to keep going.

- Muscle cells work as a team—getting stronger, increasing performance, pumping blood back to heart.

- Mental concentration increases.

- Your spirit is unleashed as you find yourself improving.

ENDORPHINS KILL PAIN, MAKE YOU FEEL GOOD

Running at any pace, but especially speed training, signals to your body that there will be some pain to kill. The natural response is to produce internal painkillers called endorphins. These hormones act as drugs that relax and deal with muscle discomfort, while bestowing a good attitude—especially when you are tired after the run. Walking during the rest interval allows the endorphins to collect—so you'll feel even better.

GRADUALLY PUSHING UP THE WORKLOAD

Your body is programmed to improve when it is gradually introduced to a little more work, with enough rest afterward. Push too hard, or neglect the rest, and you'll see an increase in aches, pains and injury. When speed workouts are balanced, adjustments are made to problems and goals are realistic, most runners can continue to improve for years.

STRESS + REST = IMPROVEMENT

When we run a little faster than our realistic goal pace, and increase the number of repetitions a little more than we did on last week's speed workout, this greater workload breaks down the muscle cells, tendons, etc. and stimulates change. You see, our bodies are programmed to rebuild stronger than before when slightly overwhelmed. But there must be gentle and regular stress, followed by significant rest to promote this regeneration.

INTRODUCING THE BODY TO SPEED THROUGH "DRILLS"

As a gentle introduction to faster running, I've found nothing better than the two drills that are detailed in the "Drills" chapter: Turnover Drills & Acceleration-Gliders. The former helps to improve cadence of the legs and feet. The latter provides a very gentle introduction to speedwork, in very short segments.

Most of the running during the conditioning period is at an easy pace. These drills, done in the middle of a short run once or twice a week, will improve mechanics, get the muscles ready for the heavier demands of speed training and initiate internal physiological changes in the muscles—with very little risk of injury.

A GENTLE INCREASE IN YOUR WEEKLY WORKOUTS CAUSES A SLIGHT BREAKDOWN

The weekly speed workout starts with a few speed repetitions, with rest between each. As the number of repetitions increase each week your body is pushed slightly beyond what it did the previous week. In each workout, your muscle fibers get tired as they reach the previous maximum workload, and continue like motivated slaves to keep you running the pace assigned. In every session some are pushed beyond their capacity with each additional speed repetition. Often, pain and fatigue are not felt during the workout. But within one or two days there are usually sore muscles and tendons, and general overall tiredness. Even walking may not feel smooth for a day or two after a speed session that is run too hard. A little bit of these symptoms is fine. When you have a lot of it—you did too much. Too much work tends to result in a negative attitude also.

THE DAMAGE

Looking inside the cell at the end of a hard workout, you'll see damage:

- Tears in the muscle cell membrane.

- The mitochondria (that process the energy inside the cell) are swollen.

- There's a significant lowering of the muscle stores of glycogen (the energy supply needed in speedwork).

- Waste products from exertion, bits of bone and muscle tissue and other bio junk can be found.

- Sometimes, there are small tears in the blood vessels and arteries, and blood leaks into the muscles.

THE DAMAGE STIMULATES THE MUSCLES AND TENDONS TO REBUILD STRONGER AND BETTER THAN BEFORE

Your body is programmed to get better when it is pushed beyond its current limits. A slight increase is better than a greater increase because the repair can be done relatively quickly.

YOU MUST HAVE ENOUGH REST IF YOU WANT TO REBUILD STRONGER AND BETTER

Two days after a speed session, if the muscles have had enough rest, you'll see some improvements:

- Waste has been removed.

- Thicker cell membranes can handle more work without breaking down.

- The mitochondria have increased in size and number, so that they can process more energy next time.

- The damage to the blood system has been repaired.

- Over several months, after adapting to a continued series of small increases, more capillaries (tiny fingers of the blood system) are produced. This improves and expands the delivery of oxygen and nutrients and provides a better withdrawal of waste products.

These are only some of the many adaptations made by the incredible human body when we do speedwork within our limits: bio-mechanics, nervous system, strength, muscle efficiency and more. Internal psychological improvements follow the physical ones. Mind, body, and spirit are becoming a team, improving health and performance. An added benefit is a positive attitude.

QUALITY REST IS CRUCIAL: 48 HOURS BETWEEN WORKOUTS

On rest days, it's important to avoid exercises that strenuously use the calf muscle, ankle and achilles tendon (stair machines, step aerobics, spinning out of the saddle) for the 48-hour period between running workouts. If you have other aches and pains from your individual "weak links" then don't do exercises that aggravate them further. Walking is usually a great exercise for a rest day. There are several other good exercises in the "Cross-Training" section of this book. As long as you are not continuing to stress the calf, most alternative exercises are fine.

BEWARE OF JUNK MILES

Those training for a time goal often develop injuries because they try to "sneak in" a few miles on the days they should be resting. Even more than running long distance, speed training stresses the feet and legs. For best recovery, don't run during the next 40 hours. The short, junk-mile days don't help your conditioning, and they keep your muscles from recovering.

REGULARITY

To maintain the adaptations, you must regularly run, about every two days. To maintain the speed improvements mentioned in this book, you should do the speed work listed in the training schedules. Acceleration-gliders and cadence drills should be done once a week and 800-meter repeats done every two weeks. It is OK to delay a workout every once in a while, but you need to stay on the schedule as close as possible. Missing two workouts in a row will result in a slight loss in the capacity you have been developing. The longer you wait, the harder it will be to start up again.

"MUSCLE MEMORY"

Your neuro-muscular system remembers the patterns of muscle activity which you have done regularly over an extended period of time. The longer you have been running regularly the more easily it will be to start up when you've had a layoff. During your first few months of speedwork, for example, if you miss a weekly workout, you will need to drop back a week, and rebuild. But if you have run regularly for several years, and you miss a speed workout, little will be lost if you start the next one very slowly, and ease into it. Be careful as you return to speed training, if this happens.

TIP: CRAMPED FOR TIME? JUST DO A FEW REPETITIONS

Let's say that you cannot get to the track on your speed day, and you don't have but 15 minutes to run. Take a 3- to 4-minute slow warm-up with some accelerations, and do the same, in reverse, during the last 3-5 minutes. During the middle 5-9 minutes, run several 1- to 2-minute accelerations at approximately the pace you would run on the track. Don't worry if the pace is not perfect. Any of these segments is better than a week without any fast running at all. Then, the following week, you can do the workout (or most of it) planned for that week.

AEROBIC RUNNING IS DONE DURING LONG RUNS

Aerobic means "in the presence of oxygen". This is the type of running you do when you feel "slow" and comfortable. When running aerobically, your muscles can get enough oxygen from the blood to process energy in the cells (burning fat in most cases). The minimal waste products produced during aerobic running can be easily removed, with no lingering buildup in the muscles.

SPEED TRAINING GETS YOU INTO THE ANAEROBIC ZONE: AN OXYGEN DEBT

Anaerobic running means running too fast or too long for you, on that day. At some point in the workout, when you reach your current limit, the muscles can't get enough oxygen to burn the most efficient fuel, fat. So they shift to the limited supply of stored sugar: glycogen. The waste products from this fuel pile up quickly in the cells, tightening the muscles and causing you to breathe heavily. You have encountered a condition called an "oxygen debt". If you keep running for too long in this anaerobic state, you will have to slow down significantly or stop. But if you are running for a realistic time goal, and are pacing yourself correctly, you should only be running anaerobically for a short period of time, at the end of each workout and race.

THE ANAEROBIC THRESHOLD

As you increase the quantity of your speed sessions, you push back your anaerobic threshold. This means that you can run a bit farther than before—each week, at the same pace, without extreme huffing and puffing. Your muscles can move your body farther and faster without going to exhaustion. Each speed workout pushes you a little bit further into the anaerobic zone. Speedwork trains body and mind to continue working at top capacity. It also tells you that you don't have to give up on performance when in this state. Coping with the stress of speedwork prepares you for the reality of the anaerobic portions of the race itself.

THE TALK TEST: HOW AEROBIC ARE YOU?

- You're aerobic—if you can talk for as long as you want with minimal huffing & puffing (h & p).

- You are mostly aerobic—if you can talk for 30 sec and then must h & p for no more than 10 seconds.

- You are approaching anaerobic threshold—if you can only talk for 10 seconds or less, then h & p for 10+ seconds.

- You're anaerobic—if you can't talk more than a few words, and are mostly h & p.

ARE YOU WORKING TOO HARD TOWARD A TIME GOAL?

When runners get too focused on specific time goals they often feel more stress and experience some negative attitude changes. At the first sign of these symptoms, back off and let mind and body get back together again.

- Running is not as enjoyable.

- You don't look forward to your runs.

- When you say something to others about your running, the statements are often negative.

- The negativity can permeate other areas of your life.

- You look on running as work instead of play.

THE PERSONAL GROWTH OF SPEED TRAINING

Instead of looking just at the times in your races, embrace the life lessons that can come from the journey of an extended speed training program. Most of your runs must have some fun in them, to help you through the challenges. Even after a hard workout, focus on how good you feel afterward, and the satisfaction from overcoming the adversity.

The reality of a speed training program is that you'll have more setbacks than victories. But you will learn more from the setbacks and they will make you a stronger runner—and a stronger person. Confronting challenges is initially tough, but leads you to some of the great treasures of the improvement process. As you dig for deeper resources you find you have more strength inside than you.

HOW SPEED TRAINING WORKS

To run faster in the race, you need to run faster in some key workouts. The faster pace of both the workouts and the TTs force the muscles, tendons, nerves, cardiovascular system, psyche, and spirit to gear up. The regularity of the workouts sets up a process that improves efficiency. You'll also search for and find new resources needed to deal with the challenges not faced before.

800-METER REPEATS ARE RUN 15 SECONDS FASTER THAN GOAL PACE

You'll see in the time goal schedules a series of 800-meter workouts on non-long-run weekends. These are best done on a track (two laps). Each should be run 15 seconds faster than you'd like to run the same distance (approximately half a mile) in your goal race. Walk for the amount recommend in the training schedules.

SUSTAINED SPEED—THROUGH AN INCREASE IN THE NUMBER OF REPETITIONS

The maximum benefit from speed sessions is at the end of the program. As you increase the number of 800-meter speed repetitions from 4 to 6 to 8 and beyond, you teach yourself how to keep going at your assigned pace, even when tired. To maintain speed when tired is the mission. The only way to prepare for this "race reality" situation is to do this during speed training. Speedwork teaches you and your legs that they can keep performing even when very tired. The result is that you won't slow down as you would before you started doing the speedwork.

LONGER RUNS MAINTAIN ENDURANCE—AND IMPROVE YOUR TIME

Your long runs will maintain or extend endurance, while you improve speed. Every week or two you'll run a very slow longer run. Many runners improve their times through this long run as much as or more than they do from speed training. Both are important for maximum improvement.

RUNNING FORM IMPROVES

Regular speed workouts stimulate your body to run more efficiently. On each workout, as you push into fatigue, your body intuitively searches for ways of continuing to move at the same pace without extraneous motion: lighter touch of the feet, direct foot lift, lower to the ground, quicker turnover. See the chapter on running form for more details.

WATCH OUT! SPEEDWORK INCREASES ACHES, PAINS, AND INJURIES

Speed training increases your chance of injury. Be sensitive to the areas on your foot, leg, muscles, etc., where you've had problems before—your weak links. Think back to the patterns of aches and pains that have caused you to reduce or stop exercise in the past. You can reduce injury risk significantly by taking a day or two off when one of these flares up, and by following the tips in the "aches and pains" chapter in this book.

Chapter 14

RACE DAY TIMETABLE

Most runners who arrive at their half marathon race are surprised at the upbeat atmosphere. If the energy could be put in a container and used in your car, you wouldn't have to buy gasoline for weeks. Almost everyone at a race is in a good mood, and the shared excitement and optimism of the start continues through the after-race party.

- If it's your first race, look for one:
- That is fun and festive
- Has refreshments
- Includes a T-shirt and other goodies
- Provides entertainment
- Has organizers who focus on average or beginning runners

If you have run a half marathon and want to run faster, here are some other factors to consider:

- Difficulty of the course—ask your resources (next section) about this. Pick a course that tends to produce fast times.

- Weather conditions—look at the average temperatures for the day on which the race is scheduled. Your best timesshould come when the temperature is below 60°F. Remember that for every 5 degrees above 60°F, you will tend to slow down by 30 sec a mile.

- Well organized—the organizers...keep things organized: accurate measurement, accurate timing (usually using "the chip" technology), no long lines, easy to register, start goes off on time, water on the course, refreshments for all—even the slowest, no major problems.

- Competitive runners like the event, and respect the organizers.

RESOURCES: WHERE TO FIND OUT ABOUT RACES

Running stores
This resource is at the top of our list because you can usually get entry forms plus some editorial comment about the race. Explain to the store folks that this is your first race, or that you're going for a fast time. Select a fun event that has a high rating in the "what to look for" section.

Friends who run
Call a friend who has run for several years. Tell him or her that you are looking for a fun, upbeat race. Go over the same categories listed above. Be sure to ask the friend for a contact number or website where you can find more information on the event, and possibly enter. As with running store folks, the editorial comments and evaluation of an event can steer you to a good experience.

Running clubs
If there is a running club or two in your area, get in touch. The officers or members can steer you in the direction of events. Running clubs may be found by doing a web search: type "running clubs (your town)". The RRCA (Road Runner's Club of America) is a national organization of neighborhood clubs. From their website, search for a club in your area.

Newspaper listings

In many newspapers, there is a listing of community sports events, in the weekend section. This comes out on Friday or Saturday in most cities, usually in the lifestyle section. Some listings can be in the sports section under "running" or "road races". You can often find these listings on the website of the newspaper.

Web searches

Just do a web search for "road races (your town)" or "half marathon (your town)". There are several event companies that serve as a registration center for many races: including *www.signmeup.com* and *www.active.com*. From these sites you can sometimes find an event in your area, research it, and then sign up.

HOW TO REGISTER

1. Online. More and more of the road running events are conducting registration online. This allows you to bypass the process of finding an entry form, and sending it in before the deadline.

2. Fill out an entry and send it in. You will need to fill out your name, address, T-shirt size, etc., and then sign the waiver form. Be sure to include a check for the entry fee.

3. Show up on race day. Because some races don't do race day registration, be sure you can do this. There is usually a penalty for waiting until the last minute—but you can see what the weather is like before you make the trek to the race.

THE LONG RUN IS THE FOUNDATION FOR YOUR FITNESS

While some runners like to do their long runs around a track, others become very bored when they run there. Running 1-2 laps at the beginning, in the middle, and at the end of the run will allow you to get a handle on how fast you are running so that you can compute your distance for the day when running off the track.

Each week or two you will be adding distance to the long run. You want to run about 3 min/mi slower than your "magic mile" predicts in the half marathon. Take the walk breaks as noted in the walk break section of this book. It is the distance covered that builds endurance—go slower.

REHEARSAL

If at all possible, run one or more of your long runs on the race course. You'll learn how to get there, where to park (or which rapid transit station to exit), and what the site is like. If you will be driving, drive into the parking area several times to make sure you understand exactly how to go where you need to park. This will help you to feel at home with the staging area on race day. Run over the last half-mile of the course at least twice. This is the most important part of the course to know. It's also beneficial to do the first part of the course to see which side of the road is best for walk breaks (sidewalks, etc.).

Visualize your lineup position. First-time half marathoners should line up at the back. If you line up too far forward you could slow down runners that are faster. You want to do this first race slowly, and have a good experience. This is most likely at the back of the pack. Because you will be taking your walk breaks, as in training, you need to stay at the side of the road. If there is sidewalk, you can use this for your walk breaks.

THE AFTERNOON BEFORE

Don't run the day before the race. You won't lose any conditioning if you take two days off from running leading up to the race. If the race has an expo or other festivities, this is often interesting. Companies in the running business have displays, shoes, clothing, books—often at sale prices. Beware of sale shoes, however. It is best to go to a good running store and go through the procedure noted in the shoe chapter to select a shoe that is designed for the type of foot you have.

Some races require you to pick up your race number, and sometimes your computer chip (explained below) the day before. Look at the website or the entry form for instructions about this. Most races allow you to pick up your materials on race day—but be sure.

RACE NUMBER

This is sometimes called a "bib number". It should be pinned on the front of the garment you'll be wearing when you cross the finish line.

COMPUTER CHIP

More and more races are using technology that electronically picks up your race number and time as you cross the finish. You must wear this chip that is usually laced on the shoes, near the top. Some companies have a velcro band that is attached to the ankle or arm. More recently, a lot of races are including this chip as part of your race bib. Read the instructions to make sure you are attaching this correctly. Be sure to turn this in after the race. The officials have volunteers to collect them, so stop and take them off your shoe, etc. There is a steep fine for those who don't turn in the chip.

THE CARBO-LOADING DINNER

Some races have a dinner the night before. At the dinner you will usually chat with runners at your table, and enjoy the evening. Don't eat much, however. Many runners assume, mistakenly, that they must eat a lot of food the night before. This is actually counterproductive. It takes at least 24 hours for most of the food you eat to be processed and useable in a race—usually longer. There is nothing you can eat the evening before a race that will help you.

But eating too much, or the wrong foods for you, can be a real problem. A lot of food in your gut, when you are bouncing up and down in a race, is stressful. A very common and embarrassing situation occurs when the gut is emptied to relieve this stress. While you don't want to starve yourself the afternoon and evening before, the best strategy is to eat small meals, and taper down the amount as you get closer to bed time. As always, it's best to have done a "rehearsal" of eating, so that you know what works, how much, when to stop eating, and what foods to avoid. The evening before your long run is a good time to work on your eating plan, and replicate the successful routine leading up to race day.

DRINKING

The day before, drink when you are thirsty. If you haven't had a drink of water or sports drink in a couple of hours, drink half a cup to a cup (4-8 oz) each hour. Don't drink a lot of fluid during the morning of the race itself. This can lead to bathroom breaks during the race.

Many races have porto-johns around the course, but some do not. It is a very common practice for runners that have consumed too much fluid that morning to find a tree or alley along the course. A common practice is to drink 6-10 oz of fluid about two hours before the race. Usually this is totally out of the system before the start.

Tip: If you practice drinking before your long runs, you can find the right amount of fluid that works best for you on race day. Stage your drinks so that you know when you will be taking potty breaks.

THE NIGHT BEFORE

Eating is optional after 6pm. If you are hungry, have a light snack that you have tested before and has not caused problems. Less is better, but don't go to bed hungry. Continue to have about 8 oz of a good electrolyte beverage like Accelerade over the two hours before you go to bed.

Alcohol is not generally recommended because the effects of this central nervous system depressant carry over to the next morning. Some runners have no trouble having one glass of wine or beer, while others are better off with none. If you decide to have a drink, I suggest that you make it one portion.

Pack your bag and lay out your clothes so that you don't have to think very much on race morning.

- Your watch, set up for the run-walk ratio you are using
- Shoes
- Socks
- Shorts
- Top—see clothing thermometer
- Pin race number on the front of the garment in which you will be finishing
- A few extra safety pins
- Water, Accelerade, pre-race and post-race beverages (such as Endurox R4), and a cooler if you wish
- Food for the drive in, and the drive home
- Bandages, Vaseline, any other first aid items you may need
- Cash for registration if you are doing race day registration (check for exact amount, including late fee)
- $25-40 for gas, food, parking, etc.
- Race chip attached according to the race instructions
- A few jokes or stories to provide laughs or entertainment before the start
- A copy of the "race day checklist", which is just below this section

SLEEP

You may sleep well, or you may not. Don't worry about it if you don't sleep at all. Many runners I work with every year don't sleep at all the night before and have the best race of their lives. Of course, don't try to go sleepless....but if it happens, it is not a problem.

RACE DAY CHECKLIST

Copy this list so that you will not only have a plan, you can carry it out in a methodical way. Pack the list in your race bag. Don't try anything new the day of your race—except for health or safety. The only item I have heard about when used for the first time in a race that has helped is the taking of walk breaks. Even first time users benefit significantly. Otherwise, stick with your plan.

Fluid and potty stops—after you wake up, drink 4-6 oz of water every half hour. If you have used Accelerade about 30 minutes before your runs, prepare it. Use a cooler if you wish. In order to avoid the bathroom stops, stop your fluid intake according to what has worked for you before.

Eat—what you have eaten before your harder runs. It is OK to not eat at all before a half marathon unless you are a diabetic, then go with the plan that you and your doctor (or nutritionist) have worked out.

Get your bearings—walk around the site to find where you want to line up (at the back of the pack, or in a pace group), and how you will get to the start. Choose a side of the road that has more shoulder or sidewalk for ease in taking walk breaks.

Register or pick up your race number—if you already have all of your materials, you can bypass this step. If not, look at the signage in the registration area and get in the right line. Usually there is one for "race day registration" and one for those who registered online or in the mail and need to pick up their numbers.

Start your warm-up 40-50 min before the start. If possible, go backwards on the course for about .5-.6 mi and turn around. This will give you a preview of the most important part of your race—the finish. Here is the warm-up routine:

- Walk for 5 minutes, slowly.

- Walk at a normal walking pace for 3-5 minutes, with a relaxed and short stride.

- Start your watch for the ratio of running and walking that you are using and do this for 10 minutes.

- Walk around for 5-10 minutes.

- If you are shooting for a time goal, do a few acceleration-gliders: 4-8 of them.

- If you have time, walk around the staging area, read your jokes, laugh, relax.

- Get in position and pick one side of the road or the other where you want to line up.

- When the road is closed, and runners are called onto the road, go to the curb and stay at the side of the road, near or at the back of the crowd (for first-timers). Time goal runners or race veterans should place themselves near the pace per mile sign in the start area, corresponding to current pace potential.

AFTER THE START

Remember that you can control how you feel during and afterward by conservative pacing and walks.

- Stick with your run/walk ratio that has worked for you—take every walk break, especially the first one.

- If it is warm, slow down and walk more.

- Don't let yourself be pulled out too fast during the running portions.

- As people pass you who don't take walk breaks, tell yourself that you will catch them later—you will.

- If anyone interprets your walking as weakness, say: "This is my proven strategy for a strong finish".

- Talk with folks along the way, enjoy the course, smile often.

- On warm days, pour water over your head at the water stops. Use the fluid plan that you've used successfully on long runs. Be sure to read the section on heat disease in this book, and don't drink more than 27 oz an hour.

AT THE FINISH

- In the upright position,
- with a smile on your face,
- wanting to do it again.

AFTER THE FINISH

- Keep walking for at least half a mile.
- Drink about 4-8 oz of fluid.
- Within 30 min of the finish, have a snack that is 80% carbohydrate/20% protein (Endurox R4 is best).
- If you can soak your legs in cool water, during the first two hours after the race, do so for 10-20 min.
- Walk for 20-30 minutes later in the day.

THE NEXT DAY

- Walk for 30-60 minutes, very easy. This can be done at one time, or in installments.
- Keep drinking about 4-6 oz an hour of water or sports drink like Accelerade.
- Wait at least a week before you either schedule your next race or vow to never run another one again.

YOUR JOURNAL WILL INSPIRE YOU

It would be wonderful if we never had to write anything down. In this magic world you could rely upon your brain to track and retain everything you do, and sort it constantly to prepare you for the next few activities. Then, moments before you were scheduled to do something, a brain transmission would arrive, telling you exactly what to do, where to do it, the materials you need, and the deadline. And while we're dreaming, this would be done with complete consistency, hour after hour, day after day.

Since we don't operate in a perfect world, with a perfect brain, a journal allows us to plan the future, track our behaviors, learn from our mistakes, and chart our progress in a consistent direction. With a simple logbook format that each of us chooses, we can see what to do, usually within a few minutes, and make the adjustments necessary. Journals give us control over our future while they allow us to learn from our past.

I'm not suggesting that everything be scheduled in advance. Some of the most inspiring moments and memorable actions sneak up on us unexpectedly. In your journal you can trap these and relive the positive feelings. But by using your journal to plan ahead, you're programming the brain to continuously steer toward interesting opportunities that arise, as you fine-tune the training and the goal. You don't even have to have a time goal to benefit from a journal. Journals are extremely helpful in ensuring that you schedule and record the enjoyable components while avoiding the stressful trends that produce injury.

Of all the activities that surround running, it is the writing and reviewing of your journal that gives the greatest control over the direction of your running so you can make adjustments. It only takes a few minutes, every other day to record the key information. Looking back through your entries will provide laughs and enjoyment. You'll revisit the interesting things you saw during the last week, the crazy thoughts, the people you met and the fun. This process can inspire the right brain to produce more entertainment, as you schedule runs that promote its activity.

JOURNAL KEEPERS ARE MORE LIKELY TO BE LIFELONG RUNNERS

Many beginning runners tell me that the writing of each day's mileage in the journal was their greatest motivation—simple but satisfying. After a few weeks, many runners learn the empowerment of organizing runs in the journal. By the time six months have passed, you'll discover the satisfaction of looking ahead several months to schedule races, the training needed for them, while ensuring that there are fun events along the way. I hear from several runners every month who use their journal as a diary, noting the other significant activities, the kids' soccer scores, and PTA notes.

Whatever format you choose, you'll find that by scheduling that very important time for yourself (the run time) in the journal, that you actually run more times per week. The journal becomes the steering wheel that keeps you on the road of positive progress. As you hold tight and use the wheel, you feel an empowering sense of making progress.

RESTORING ORDER

One runner told me "When my wife died, and my life seemed to be in chaos, I felt a simple and powerful sense of security in documenting the distance that I covered each day. No one could take that away from me." Another runner commented: "As a young executive and a young Mom I felt that I had no control over my life until I started using a training journal. It started with writing distance, then temperature, pace and route. My journal writing time was the only part of my day when I felt I had control. It was wonderful!"

A SIMPLE REWARD CAN PULL YOU OUT OF THE DUMPS

We all feel better and enjoy our activities when we feel rewarded. The simple act of recording the distance you cover each day will give you a genuine sense of accomplishment that is felt internally. When you string together a series of runs on days you didn't feel like running, you feel so good inside. Even the most upbeat people have periods of low motivation, and have told me that their journals got them re-focused on the down days.

THIS IS YOUR BOOK

Yes, you are writing a book. At the most basic, you will have an outline of your running life during the next few months. No one tells you what goes into this book. As runners record their entries in the log, they realize that they can use the same journal to organize other areas of life. Even runners who are not fired up about the process at first are usually impressed at how many benefits flow from this tool. Since you don't need to show anyone your journal, you can let your feelings go as you write. Upon review, your emotional response to a given workout can be very interesting months or years later.

CAN YOU CAPTURE THE FLEETING THOUGHTS OF THE RIGHT BRAIN?

One of the interesting challenges, and great rewards, of journaling is noting the creative and sometimes crazy images that emerge from the right side of our head. On some days you won't get any of these, and on others...the faucet opens up. Often the thoughts come out of nowhere. Other times, you will be suddenly hit with a solution to a problem you've been working on for months. If you have your journal available at the place where you return from your run—car, office desk, kitchen countertop—you can quickly jot some key words to describe the images or craziness.

THE VARIOUS TYPES OF JOURNALS

Calendar—facing you on the wall

Many runners start recording their runs on a wall calendar—or one that is posted on the refrigerator. Looking at the miles recorded is empowering. But equally motivating for many is avoiding too many "zeros" on days that should have been running days. If you're not sure whether you will really get into this journal process, you may find it easiest to start with a calendar.

This is a page from *Jeff Galloway's Training Journal*:

Week of | Jan 1

Thursday — Jan 4

GOAL	35 min easy (sc)	
TIME	45 min	
DISTANCE	@ 6.5	
AM PULSE	49	
WEATHER	Cloudy	
TEMP	40°	
TIME	6	AM/PM
TERRAIN	rolling	
WALK BREAK	—	

COMMENTS (1-10)

Great run with Barb, Wes + Sambo — who took out the pace too fast + died at the end. The rest of us caught up on the gossip. Achilles ached so I iced it for 15 minutes.

Friday — Jan 5

GOAL	45 min (sp) 5 × 800 meter	
TIME	1:15	
DISTANCE	7.5 mi	
AM PULSE	53	
WEATHER	45°	
TEMP	Sunny	
TIME	5	AM/PM
TERRAIN	track	
WALK BREAK	400 m	

COMMENTS

2:30
2:36
2:33
2:37
2:32
2:36

My best workout in years!
- walked 400m between each
- struggled on last one

Achilles ached - iced 15 min

12min warm up and warm down

Saturday — Jan 6

GOAL	Off	
TIME		
DISTANCE		
AM PULSE	55	
WEATHER		
TEMP		
TIME		AM/PM
TERRAIN		
WALK BREAK		

COMMENTS

Kids soccer (morn)
* Westin scores goal bouncing off his back
1st goal of season!
Brennan's cross country (aft)
Invitational
* Brennan comes from 8th to 3rd in the last half mile. I'm so proud!

Sunday — Jan 7

GOAL	18 mi easy! (1)	
TIME	2:53	
DISTANCE	18 mi	
AM PULSE	52	
WEATHER	50°	
TEMP	dry no wind	
TIME		AM/PM
TERRAIN	flat	
WALK BREAK	1 min / mi	

COMMENTS

It was great to cover 18 miles — wish I had a group
longest run in 18 months!
but...
* went too fast in the first 5 miles
* Achilles hurt afterward - take 3 days off
* Power Bar + water from 10mi kept spirits up

← Pulse is up — I'm not recovering — need more days off/week

An organized running journal

When you use a product that is designed for running, you don't have to think to record the facts. The spaces on the page ask you for certain info, and you will learn to fill it very quickly. This leaves you time to use some of the open space for the creative thoughts and ideas that pop out during a run. Look at the various journals available and pick one that looks to be easier to use, and to carry with you. I've included a sample page of my Jeff Galloway's Training Journal as one example.

Notebook

You don't need to have a commercial product. You can create your own journal by using a basic school notebook of your choice. Find one in a size that works best with your lifestyle (briefcase, purse, etc.) Below you will find the items that I've found helpful for most runners to record. But the best journals are those that make it easier for you to collect the data you find interesting, while allowing for creativity. The non-limiting nature of a notebook is a more comfortable format for runners that like to write a lot one day, and not so much another day.

Computer logs

There are a growing number of software products that allow you to sort through information more quickly. As you set up your own codes and sections you can pick data that is important to you, sort it to see trends and plan ahead. Some software allows for you to download data from a heart monitor or GPS or smartwatch.

THE WRITING PROCESS

1. Capturing the flow from the right brain

    Try to have the log handy so that you can record info after a run. Immediately after a run, you will have fresh perceptions, and will be more likely to record the right brain images and thoughts that tend to fade quickly.

2. Just the facts

    At first, spend a few seconds and quickly jot down the key info that you want recorded. If you have to think about an item, skip it and just fill in the items you can fill in quickly. Here is a list of items that many runners use:

- Date:
- Morning pulse:
- Time of run:
- Distance covered:
- Time running:
- Weather:
- Temperature:
- Precipitation:
- Humidity:

Comments:

- Walk-Run frequency
- Any special segments of the run (speed, hills, race, etc.)
- Running companion
- Terrain
- How did you feel (1-10)

3. Go back over the list again and fill in more details—emotional responses, changes in energy or blood sugar level, and location of places where you had aches and pains—even if they went away during the run. You are looking for patterns of items that could indicate injury, blood sugar problems, lingering fatigue, etc.

4. Helpful additions (usually in a blank section at the bottom of the page)

- Improvement thoughts
- Things I should have done differently
- Interesting happenings
- Funny things
- Strange things
- Stories, right brain crazy thoughts

ARE YOU TIRED...OR JUST LAZY? YOUR MORNING PULSE MAY TELL

Many people say that they are too tired to run. But after interviewing many who make this claim, I've come to believe that most of the reasons for this sensation is laziness (most will admit this), or low blood sugar. One of the best indicators of real fatigue is your resting pulse, taken in the morning. Your journal can track this (although some runners use a piece of graph paper).

Recording morning pulse

1. As soon as you are conscious—but before you have thought much about anything—count your pulse rate for a minute. Record it before you forget it. If you don't have your journal by your bed, then keep a piece of paper and pen handy.

2. It is natural for there to be some fluctuation, based upon the time you wake up, how long you have been awake, etc. But after several weeks and months, these will balance themselves out. Try to catch the pulse at the instant that you are awake, before the shock of an alarm clock, thoughts of work stress, etc.

3. After 2 weeks or so of readings, you can establish a base line morning pulse. Take out the top 2 high readings and then compute an average.

4. The average is your guide. If the rate is 5% higher than your average, take an easy day. When the rate is 10% higher, and there is no reason for this (you woke up from an exciting dream, medication, infection, etc.) then your muscles may be tired indeed. Take the day off if you have a run scheduled for that day.

5. If your pulse stays high for more than a week, call your doctor to see if there is a reason for this (medication, infection, hormones, metabolic changes, etc.).

Chapter 16

RUNNING FORM

I believe that running is an inertia activity: your mission is simply to maintain momentum. Very little strength is needed to run. The first few strides get you into motion, and your focus thereafter is to stay in motion. To reduce fatigue, aches and pains, your body intuitively fine-tunes your motion so that you minimize effort, as you continue to run about every other day, month after month.

Humans have many biomechanical adaptations for running and walking, which have been made more efficient over more than a million years. The anatomical origin of efficiency in humans is the combination of the calf muscle, ankle and the achilles tendon. This is an extremely sophisticated system of levers, springs, balancing devices and more, involving hundreds of component parts amazingly well coordinated. Biomechanics experts believe that this degree of development was not needed for walking. When our ancient ancestors had to run to survive, the evolution reached a new level of performance.

When we have the right balance of walking and running, very little effort from the calf muscle produces a smooth continuation of forward movement. As the calf muscle gets in better shape, and improves endurance, you can keep going, mile after mile, with little perceived effort. Other muscle groups offer support and fine-tune the process. When you feel aches and pains that might be due to the way you run, going back to the minimal use of the ankle and achilles tendon can often leave you feeling smooth and efficient very quickly.

A BETTER WAY OF RUNNING?

There may be a better way to run for you, one that will leave your legs with more strength and result in fewer aches and pains. The fact is, however, that most runners are not far from great efficiency. Repeated research on runners has shown that most are running very close to their ideal. I believe this is due to the action of the right brain. After tens of thousands of steps, it keeps searching for (and refining) the most efficient pattern of feet, legs, and body alignment.

In my full-day running schools and weekend retreats I conduct an individual running form analysis with each runner. After having analyzed more than 10,000 runners, I've also found that most are running in a very efficient way. The problems are seldom big ones—but a series of small mistakes. By making a few minor adjustments, most runners can feel better on every run.

THE BIG THREE: POSTURE, STRIDE, AND BOUNCE

In these consultations, I've also discovered that when runners have problems, they tend to occur in three areas: posture, stride, and bounce. And the problems tend to be individual in nature. They occur most often in specific areas because of specific motions. Fatigue increases the irritation of the "weak link" areas. A slight overstride, for example creates fatigue and then a feeling of weakness at the end of a run. As a tired body "wobbles", other muscle groups try to keep it on course, but are not designed for this.

THREE NEGATIVE RESULTS OF INEFFICIENT FORM

1. Fatigue becomes so severe that it takes much longer to recover.

2. Muscles are pushed so far beyond their limits that they break down and become injured.

3. The experience is so negative, that the desire to run is reduced, producing burnout.

Almost everyone has some slight problem. The goal is not to have perfect running form. But when you become aware of your form problems, and make changes to keep them from producing aches and pains, you'll experience smoother running and faster times. This chapter can help you understand why aches and pains tend to come out of form problems—and how you may be able to reduce or eliminate them.

YOUR OWN FORM CHECK

In some of my clinics, I take photos for instant feedback. Have a friend take pictures of you running, from the side (not running toward or away from the camera) while you run on a flat surface. Some runners can check themselves while running alongside stores that offer a reflection in a plate glass window. The sections below will tell you what to look for.

IF YOU FEEL RELAXED AND RUNNING IS EASY EVEN AT THE END OF A RUN, YOU'RE PROBABLY RUNNING CORRECTLY

Overall, the running motion should feel easy. There should be no tension in your neck, back, shoulders or legs. A good way to correct problems is to change posture, foot or leg placement so running is easier and there is no tightness or pain.

POSTURE

Good running posture is actually good body posture. The head is naturally balanced over the shoulders, which are aligned over the hips. As the foot comes underneath, all of these elements are in balance so that no energy is needed to prop up the body. You shouldn't have to work to pull a wayward body back from a wobble or inefficient motion.

Forward lean

The posture errors tend to be mostly due to a forward lean—especially when we are tired. The head wants to get to the finish as soon as possible, but the legs can't go any faster. In their first races, beginners are often the ones whose heads are literally ahead of the body, which produces more than a few falls around the finish line. A forward lean will often concentrate fatigue, soreness and tightness in the lower back or neck.

It all starts with the head. When the neck muscles are relaxed, the head is usually in a natural position. If there is tension in the neck, or soreness afterward, the head is usually leaning too far forward. This triggers a more general upper body imbalance in which the head and chest are suspended slightly ahead of the hips and feet. Ask a running companion to tell you if and when your head is too far forward, or leaning down. The ideal position of the head is mostly upright, with your eyes focused about 30-40 yards ahead of you.

Sitting back

The hips are the other major postural area where runners can get out of alignment. A runner with this problem, when observed from the side, will have the butt behind the rest of the body. When the pelvis area is shifted back, the legs are not allowed to go through a natural range of motion, and the stride length becomes short. This results in a slower pace, even when spending significant effort. Many runners tend to hit harder on their heels when their hips are shifted back.

A backward lean is rare

It is rare for runners to lean back, but it happens. In my experience, this is usually due to a structural problem in the spine or hips. If you do this, and you're having pain in the neck, back or hips, you should see an orthopedist.

Correction: "Puppet on a string"

The best correction I've found to postural problems has been this mental exercise: imagine that you are a puppet on a string. Suspended from up above like a puppet—from the head and each side of the shoulders—your head lines up with the shoulders, the hips come directly underneath, and the feet naturally touch lightly. It won't hurt anyone to do the "puppet" several times during a run. It helps to combine this image with a deep breath. About every 4-5 minutes, as you start to run after a walk break, take a deep, lower lung breath, straighten up and say "I'm a puppet". Then imagine that you don't have to spend energy maintaining this upright posture, because the strings attached from above keep you on track. As you continue to do this, you reinforce good posture, as you produce a good "habit".

Upright posture not only allows you to stay relaxed, you will probably improve your stride length. When you lean forward, you shorten your stride to stay balanced. When you straighten up, you'll receive a stride bonus of an inch or so, without any increase in energy. Note: Don't try to increase stride length. If it happens by a posture improvement, it will occur naturally.

An oxygen dividend

Breathing improves when you straighten up. A leaning body can't get ideal use out of the lower lungs. This can cause side pain. When you run upright the lower lungs can receive adequate air, absorb oxygen better, and you'll reduce the chance of side pain.

Feet low to the ground

The most efficient stride is a shuffle—with feet right next to the ground. As long as you pick your foot up enough to avoid stumbling over a rock or uneven pavement, stay low to the ground. Most runners don't need more than one-inch clearance.

Your ankle combined with your achilles tendon will act as a spring, moving you forward. If you stay low to the ground, very little effort is required. Through this "shuffling" technique, running becomes almost automatic. When runners err on bounce, they try to push off too hard. This usually results in extra effort spent in lifting the body off the ground. You can think of this as energy wasted in the air—energy that could be used to run another mile or two.

The other negative effect of a higher bounce is that of gravity. The higher you rise, the harder you will fall. Each additional bounce off the ground delivers a lot more impact on feet and legs—which on long runs produces aches, pains and injuries.

The correction for too much bounce: Light touch

You should touch so lightly that you don't usually feel yourself pushing off or landing. This means that your foot stays low to the ground and goes though an efficient and natural motion. Instead of trying to overcome gravity, you get in synch with it.

Here's a "light touch drill": During the middle of a run, time yourself for 20 seconds. Focus on one item: touching so softly that you don't hear your feet. Earplugs are not allowed for this drill. Imagine that you are running on thin ice or through a bed of hot coals. Do several of these 20 second touches, becoming quieter and quieter. You should feel very little impact on your feet as you do this drill.

Stride length

Studies have shown that as runners get faster, the stride length generally shortens. This clearly shows that the key to faster and more efficient running is increased cadence or turnover of feet and legs.

A major cause of aches, pains and injuries is a stride length that is too long. At the end of this chapter you'll see a list of problems and how to correct them. When in doubt, it is always better to err on the side of having a shorter stride.

Don't lift your knees!

Even world-class distance runners don't do this, because it tires the quadriceps muscle (front of the thigh), leading to a stride that is too long to be efficient. The most common time when runners stride too long is at the end of a tiring run. This slight overstride when the legs are tired will leave your quads (front of thigh) sore the next day or two.

Don't kick out too far in front of you!

If you watch the natural movement of the leg, it will kick forward slightly as the foot gently moves forward in the running motion to contact the ground. Let this be a natural motion that produces no tightness in the muscles behind the lower or upper leg.

Tightness in the front of the shin, or behind the knee, or in the hamstring (back of the thigh) is a sign that you are kicking too far forward. Correct this by staying low to the ground, shortening the stride, and lightly touching the ground.

CADENCE OR TURNOVER DRILL

This easy drill improves your efficiency, making it easier for you to run. This drill excels in helping you to pull all the elements of good running form together at the same time. Over the weeks and months, if you do this drill once every week, you will find that your normal cadence slowly increases naturally.

1. Warm up by walking for 5 minutes, and running and walking very gently for 10 minutes.

2. Start jogging slowly for 1-2 minutes, and time yourself for 30 seconds. During this half-minute, count the number of times your left foot touches the ground.

3. Walk around for a minute or so.

4. On the next 30-second drill, increase the count by 1 or 2.

5. Repeat this 3-7 more times. Each time trying to increase by 1-2 additional counts.

In the process of improving turnover, the body's internal monitoring system coordinates a series of adaptations which pulls together all of the form components into an efficient team:

- Your foot touches more gently.

- Extra, inefficient motions of the foot and leg are reduced or eliminated.

- Less effort is spent on pushing up or pushing forward.

- You stay lower to the ground.

- The ankle becomes more efficient.

- Ache and pain areas are not overused.

WALKING FORM

Walking form is usually not an issue when walking at a gentle, strolling pace. But every year, there are runners who get injured because they are walking in a way that aggravates some area of the foot or leg. Most of these problems come from trying to walk too fast, with too long a stride, or from using a race walking (or power walking) technique.

1. Avoid a long walking stride. Maintain a relaxed, motion that does not stress the knees, tendons or muscles of the leg, feet, knees or hips. If you feel pain or aggravation in these areas, shorten your stride. Many runners find that they can learn to walk fairly fast with a short stride. But when in doubt, use the walk for recovery and ease off.

2. Don't lead with your arms. Minimal arm swing is best. Swinging the arms too much can encourage a longer walk stride which can push into aches and pains quickly. The extra rotation produced can also aggravate hips, shoulder and neck areas. You want the legs to set the rhythm for your walk and your run. When this happens you are more likely to get into the "zone" of the right brain.

3. Let your feet move the way that is natural for them. When runners or walkers try techniques that supposedly increase stride length by landing farther back on the heel or pushing farther on the toe (than is natural for the individual), many get injured.

Chapter 17

LOWERING BODY FAT CAN HELP YOU RUN FASTER

With less fat on your body, you will feel better running, and can run faster. It is possible to burn fat while training for a half marathon, but you need to ensure you're recovering fast enough. The concepts in this chapter can help you add to the fat burning while you train for your goal. But you should back off on these if you're not recovering.

FAT-BURNING PRIORITIES

1. Top priority workouts—be sure to do these each week.

2. Second priority workouts—it would be very beneficial to do these each week.

3. Do these if you have time—they will help, just have a lower priority.

Days of the week are listed only as a suggestion. Feel free to adjust to your schedule. If you cannot do the total length of the session, do whatever you can—even 10 minutes is better than nothing. Walking is a great way to burn extra calories on a running or a non-running day. Using a step counter will allow you to break up the walking into an all day series of step segments. See the section on 10,000 steps a day.

Sunday (1)

Run the distance scheduled for a long run. If you walk more and go slowly enough, you could increase a quarter to a half-mile more on each long one than is on the schedule. Don't be afraid to put more walking in the beginning. The mission here is to keep going while feeling good. You should finish each long one knowing that you could have run farther.

Monday (3)

Do one or more alternative exercise(s) that raises body temperature, while allowing you to continue for 60+ minutes. Even on time-crunched days, try to shoot for 45 minutes. Even if you can only squeeze in 15 minutes, the extra calories burned will help in total fat burning for the week. Stair machine work is not recommended. If you have to break up these exercises into 5-15 min segments—do it.

Tuesday (1)

A moderate run of 45-60 minutes. These shorter runs allow you to maintain the fat-burning adaptations gained in the longer one on the weekend. These could be done at whatever pace you wish, but when in doubt, go slower—and go longer.

Wednesday (3)

Alternative exercise, same as Monday: 60 minutes

Thursday (1)

Same as Tuesday: 45-60 minutes

Friday (3)

Alternative exercise, same as Monday: 60 minutes

Saturday (3)

You can have this day off if you wish. Because it is the day before your long one, it's best to take it very easy. If you do any exercise, a short and gentle walk would be fine, but you need fresh muscles for the long one.

HOW MUCH WALKING AND HOW MUCH RUNNING?

Follow the guidelines in the chapter on the run-walk-run method. In the beginning, you may be running a few seconds and walking for 1-2 minutes. Very gradually you will increase the amount of running. Don't push too quickly. It would be better to choose a ratio that seems too easy for you.

10,000 MORE STEPS A DAY ON NON-RUNNING DAYS/6,000 ON RUNNING DAYS

A pedometer, or step counter, can change you into a constant fat-burner. This device gives you an incentive and reinforcement for adding extra steps to your day. It also gives you a sense of control over your actual calorie burn off. Once you get into the practice of taking more than 10,000 steps a day in your everyday activities, you find yourself getting out of your chair more often, parking farther away from the supermarket, walking around the kid's playground, practice field, etc.

These devices are usually about one inch square, and clip onto your belt, pocket or waistband. The inexpensive models just count steps and this is all you need. Other models compute miles and calories. I recommend getting one from a quality manufacturer. When tested, some of the really inexpensive ones registered 3-4 times as many steps as the quality products did—walking exactly the same course.

Your goal is to accumulate 10,000 steps at home, at work, going shopping, waiting for kids, etc. on your non-running days, and 6,000 on your running days. This is very doable. You will find many pockets of time during the day when you are just sitting or standing. When you use these to add steps to your day, you burn fat and feel better. You become a very active person.

About dinnertime you should do a "step check". If you haven't acquired your 10,000 (or 6,000), walk around the block a few extra times after dinner. You don't have to stop with these figures. As you get into it, you'll find many more opportunities to walk...and burn.

15-30 POUNDS OF FAT...GONE

Depending upon how many times you do the following each week, you have many opportunities each day to burn a little here, and a little there. These are easy movements that don't produce tiredness, aches or pains, but at the end of the year—it really adds up:

Pounds per year	Activity
1-2	taking the stairs instead of the elevator
10-30	getting out of your chair at work to walk down the hall
5-10	getting off the couch to move around the house (but not to get potato chips)
1-2	parking farther away from the super-market, mall, etc.
1-3	parking farther away from your work
2-4	walking around the kids' playground, practice field (chasing the kids)
2-4	walking up and down the concourse as you wait for your next flight
3-9	walking the dog each day
2-4	walking a couple of times around the block after supper
2-4	walking a couple of times around the block during lunch hour at work
2-4	walking an extra loop around the mall, supermarket, etc. to look for bargains (this last one could be expensive when at the mall)
Total: 31-76 pounds a year	

15 MORE POUNDS BURNED EACH YEAR FROM ADDING A FEW EXTRA MILES A DAY

By wisely using those small pockets of time that exist in every day, you can add to your fat-burning without feeling extra fatigue:

- Slow down and go one more mile on each run.

- Walk a mile at lunchtime.

- Jog a mile before dinner, or afterward.

Chapter 18

FAT BURNING: THE INCOME SIDE OF THE EQUATION

Gaining control over your calorie intake is crucial for body fat reduction. Runners often complain that even though they have increased mileage, and faithfully done their cross-training workouts, they are not losing weight. When I have questioned them, each did not have a handle on the amount of calories they were eating. In every case, when they went through the drill of quantifying, each was eating more than they thought. Below you will find ways to take 10 or more pounds off your body—without starving yourself.

WEBSITES TELL YOU CALORIE BALANCE AND NUTRIENT BALANCE

The best tool I've found for managing your food intake is a good website or software program. There are a number of these that will help to balance your calorie bottom line (calories burned vs calories eaten). Most of these will have you log in your exercise for the day, and what you eat. At the end of the day, you can retrieve an account of calories, and of nutrients. If you are low on certain vitamins or minerals, protein, etc., after dinner, you can eat food or a vitamin pill. Some programs will tell vegetarians whether they have received enough complete protein, since this nutrient is harder to put together from vegetable sources. If you haven't received enough of some nutrient, you can do something about it that night, or the next morning to make up the deficit. If you ate too many calories, walk after dinner or boost tomorrow's workouts, or reduce the calories, or both. For information on current websites visit www.JeffGalloway.com. It helps to try several before choosing one.

I don't recommend letting any website control your nutritional life until the end of your days. At first, it helps to use it every day for 1-2 weeks. During this time, you'll see patterns, and note where you tend to need supplementation or should cut back. Every week or two, do a spot check during 2-3 days. Some folks need more spot checks than others. If you're more motivated to eat the right foods and quantities by logging in every day, go for it.

PORTION CONTROL THROUGH LOGGING YOUR FOOD INTAKE

Whether you use a website or not, a very productive drill is that of logging what you eat every day, for a week. Bring a little notepad, and a small scale if you need it. As people log in, and then analyze the calories in each portion (which for most foods is about the size of a fist), they are almost always surprised at the number of calories they are eating. The fat content is often another surprise. Many foods have the fat so well disguised that you don't realize how much you are eating.

After doing this drill for several days you start to adjust the amount that you eat each meal. You are becoming the captain of your nutritional ship! Many runners have told me that they resented the first week of logging in, but it became fairly routine after that. Once you get used to doing this, you become aware of what you will be putting in your mouth, and are more likely to gradually change your eating behaviors.

EATING EVERY 2 HOURS

As mentioned in the previous chapter, if you have not eaten for about three hours, your body senses that it is going into a starvation mode, reducing the metabolism rate while increasing the production of fat-depositing enzymes. This means that you will not be burning as many calories as is normal, that you won't be as mentally and physically alert, and that more of your next meal will be stored away as fat.

If the starvation reflex starts working after 3 hours, then you can beat it by eating every 2 hours. This is a great way to burn more calories. A person who now eats 2-3 times a day, can burn about 8-10 pounds a year more when he or she shifts to eating 8-10 times a day. This assumes that the same calories are eaten every day, in the same foods.

BIG MEALS SLOW YOU DOWN

Big meals are a big production for the digestive system. Blood is diverted to the long and winding intestine and the stomach. Because of the workload, the body tends to shut down blood flow to other areas, leaving you feeling more lethargic and sedentary. Exercising muscles will be deprived of oxygen after a big meal as the blood surrounds the gut during digestion.

SMALL MEALS SPEED YOU UP

Smaller amounts of food can usually be processed quickly without putting a burden on the digestive system. Each time you eat a small meal or snack, your metabolism speeds up. Revving up the metabolism, several times a day means "more calories burned".

YOU ALSO GIVE A SETBACK TO YOUR SET POINT

When you wait more than three hours between meals the set point engages the starvation reflex. But if you eat every 2-3 hours, the set point is not engaged—due to the regular supply of food. Therefore the fat depositing enzymes don't have to be stimulated.

MOTIVATION INCREASES WHEN YOU EAT MORE OFTEN

The most common reason I've found for low motivation in the afternoon is not eating regularly enough during the day—especially during the afternoon. If you have not eaten for 4 hours or more, and you're scheduled for a run that afternoon, you will not feel very motivated—because of low blood sugar and low metabolism. Even when you have had a bad eating day, and feel down in the dumps, you can gear up for a run-walk by having a snack 30-60 minutes before exercise. A fibrous energy bar with a cup of coffee (tea, diet drink) can reverse the negative mindset. But you don't have to get yourself into this situation if you eat every 2-3 hours.

SATISFACTION FROM A SMALL MEAL TO AVOID OVEREATING

The number of calories you eat per day can be reduced by choosing foods and combinations of foods that leave you satisfied longer. Sugar is the worst problem in calorie control and satisfaction. When you drink a beverage with sugar in it, the sugar will be processed very quickly, and you will often be hungry within 30 minutes—even after consuming a high quantity of calories. This will usually lead to two undesirable outcomes:

1. Eating more food to satisfy hunger.

2. Being hungry and triggering the starvation reflex.

Your mission is to find the right combination of foods in your small meals that will leave you satisfied for 2-3 hours. Then eat another snack that will do the same. You will find a growing number of food combinations that probably have fewer calories, but keep you from getting hungry until your next snack.

NUTRIENTS THAT LEAVE YOU SATISFIED LONGER

FAT

Fat will leave you satisfied from a small meal because it slows down digestion, but a little goes a long way. When the fat content of a meal goes beyond 30%, you start to feel more lethargic due to the fact that fat is harder to digest. While a meal composed of up to about 18% of the calories in fat will help you hold hunger at bay, meals with a higher percentage of fat can compromise a fat-burning program. Fat is automatically deposited on your body. None of the dietary fat is used for energy. When you eat a fatty meal, you might as well inject it onto your hips or stomach. The fat you burn as fuel must be broken down from the stored fat on your body. The bottom line: a little fat with a snack can keep you satisfied longer, but a lot of it will mean more fat on your body.

There are two kinds of fat that have been found to cause narrowing of the arteries around the heart and leading to your brain: saturated fat and trans fat. Mono- and unsaturated fats, from vegetable sources, are usually healthy—olive oil, nuts, avocado, safflower oil. Some fish oils have omega-3 fatty acids which have been shown to have a protective effect on the heart. Many fish have oil that is not protective.

Look carefully at the labels because a lot of foods have vegetable oils that have been processed into trans fat. A wide range of baked goods and other foods have trans fat. It helps to check the labels and call the 800 number on the package to find out fat composition. The simplest solution is to avoid the food.

PROTEIN—LEAN PROTEIN IS BEST

This nutrient is needed every day for rebuilding the muscle that we break down during daily exercise and normal wear and tear. Runners, even those who log high mileage, don't need to eat significantly more protein than sedentary people. But if runners don't get their usual amount of protein, they feel more aches and pains, and general weakness, sooner than average people.

Having protein with each meal will make you feel satisfied for a longer period of time. But eating more protein calories than you need will produce a conversion of the excess into fat.

Recently, protein has been added to sports drinks with great success. When a drink with 80% carbohydrate and 20% protein (such as Accelerade) is consumed within 30 minutes of the start of a run, glycogen is activated better, and energy is supplied sooner and better. By consuming a drink that has the same ratio (like Endurox R4) within 30 minutes of finishing a run, the reloading of the muscles has been shown to be more complete.

COMPLEX CARBOHYDRATES GIVE YOU A "DISCOUNT" AND A "GRACE PERIOD"

The fiber in foods such as celery, beans, cabbage, spinach, turnip greens, grape nuts, whole grain cereal, etc., can force the digestive system to burn up to 25% of the calories in digestion. As opposed to fat (which is directly deposited on your body after eating it) it is only the excess carbs that are processed into fat. A common "grace period burnoff" to eliminate fat storage is an after-dinner walk.

FAT + PROTEIN + COMPLEX CARBS = SATISFACTION

Eating a snack that has a variety of the three satisfaction ingredients above will lengthen the time that you'll feel satisfied—even after some very small meals. These three items take longer to digest, and therefore keep the metabolism rate revved up.

OTHER IMPORTANT NUTRIENTS...

FIBER

When fiber is put into foods, it slows down digestion and maintains the feeling of satisfaction longer. Soluble fiber, such as oat bran, seems to bestow a longer feeling of satisfaction than insoluble fiber such as wheat bran. But any type of fiber will help in some way.

RECOMMENDED PERCENTAGES OF THE THREE NUTRIENTS

There are differing opinions on this issue. Here are the ranges given by a number of top nutritionists that I have read and asked. These are listed in terms of the percentage per day of each of the calories consumed in each nutrient, compared to the total number of calories per day.

Protein	between 20% and 30%
Fat	between 15% and 25%
Carbohydrate	whatever is left—hopefully in complex carbohydrates

SIMPLE CARBS HELP US PUT WEIGHT BACK ON THE BODY

We're going to eat some simple carbohydrates. These are the "feel good" foods: candy, baked sweets, starches like mashed potatoes and rice, sugar drinks (including fruit juice and sports drinks) and most desserts. When you are on a fat-burning mission, however, you need to minimize the amount of these foods.

The sugar in these products is digested so quickly that you get little or no lasting satisfaction from them. They often leave you with a craving for more. If you deprive yourself of foods you really like, you'll activate the psychological side of the starvation reflex. Because simple carbs are processed quickly, you become hungry relatively quickly and will eat, accumulating extra calories that usually end up as fat at the end of the day.

As mentioned in the last chapter, it is never a good idea to totally eliminate the decadent foods you love and say "I'll never eat another". This sets up a starvation reflex time bomb ticking. Keep taking a bite or two of the foods you dearly love, while cultivating the taste of foods with more fiber and little or no refined sugar or starch.

Chapter 19

GOOD BLOOD SUGAR = MOTIVATION

The blood sugar level (BSL) determines how good you feel. When it is at a good, moderate, regular level you feel good, stable and motivated. If you eat too much sugar, your BSL can rise too high. You'll feel really good for a while, but the excess sugar triggers a release of insulin. This usually causes a lowering of the BSL—to an uncomfortable level. In this state you don't have energy, mental focus is foggy, and motivation goes down rapidly.

When blood sugar level is maintained throughout the day, you will be more motivated to exercise, and feel like adding other movement to your life. You'll have a more positive mental attitude, and be more likely to deal with stress and solve problems. Just as eating throughout the day keeps metabolism up, the steady infusion of balanced nutrients all day long will also maintain stable blood sugar. This produces a stable feeling of well-being.

You don't want to get on the "bad side" of your BSL. Low levels are a stress on the system and literally mess with your mind. Your brain is fed by blood sugar and when the supply goes down, your mental stress goes up. If you have not eaten for several hours before a run-walk, you'll receive an increase in the number of negative messages telling you don't have the energy to exercise, that it will hurt, etc.

The simple act of eating a snack that has mostly carbohydrate and about 20% protein will reduce the negative, make you feel good and get you out the door. Keeping a snack as a BSL booster can often be the difference in running that day, or not.

THE BSL ROLLER COASTER

Eating a snack with too many calories of simple carbohydrate can be counter-productive for BSL maintenance. As mentioned above, when the sugar level gets too high, your body produces insulin, sending BSL lower than before. The tendency is to eat again, which produces excess calories that are converted into fat. But if you don't eat, you'll stay hungry and pretty miserable—in no mood to exercise or move around and burn calories or get in your run for the day.

EATING EVERY 2-3 HOURS IS BEST

Once it is established which snacks work best to maintain your BSL, most people maintain a stable blood sugar level by eating small meals regularly, every 2-3 hours. As noted in the previous chapter, it's best to combine complex carbs with protein and a small amount of fat.

DO I HAVE TO EAT BEFORE RUNNING?

Only if your blood sugar is low. Most who run-walk in the morning don't need to eat anything before the start. As mentioned above, if your blood sugar level is low in the afternoon, and you have a run scheduled, a snack can help when taken about 30 minutes before the run. If you feel that a morning snack will help, the only issue is to avoid consuming so much that you get an upset stomach.

For best results in raising blood sugar when it is too low (within 30 minutes before a run) a snack should have about 80% of the calories in simple carbohydrate and 20% in protein. This promotes the production of insulin which is helpful before a run in getting the glycogen in your muscles ready for use. The product Accelerade has worked best among the thousands of runners I hear from every year. It has the 80%/20% ratio of carb to protein. If you eat an energy bar with the 80/20 ratio, be sure to drink 6-8 oz of water with it.

EATING DURING EXERCISE

Most exercisers don't need to worry about eating or drinking during a run until the length exceeds 90 minutes. At this point, there are several options. In this case, most runners wait until the 30- to 40-minute mark in the workout before starting to take the blood sugar booster. Diabetics may need to eat sooner and more often—but this is an individual issue.

Gel-type products—These come in small packets, and are the consistency of honey or thick syrup. The most successful way to take them is to put 1-3 packets in a small plastic bottle with a pop-top. About every 10-15 minutes, take a small amount with a sip or two of water. Most runners I've heard from find it best not to take the whole packet at once.

Energy bars—Cut into 8-10 pieces and take 1-2 pieces, with a couple of sips of water, every 10-15 minutes.

Candy—particularly gummi bears or hard candies. The usual consumption is 1-3 about every 10 minutes.

Sports drinks—Since there is significant percentage of nausea among those who drink during exercise, this is not my top recommendation. If you have found this to work for you, use it exactly as you have used it before. A sports drink like Accelerade is helpful the day before or after a strenuous run. During a run, I recommend water.

IT IS IMPORTANT TO RE-LOAD AFTER EXERCISE—WITHIN 30 MINUTES

Whenever you have finished a hard or long workout (for you), a recovery snack will help you recover faster. Again, the 80/20 ratio of carb to protein has been most successful in reloading the muscles. The product that has worked best among the thousands I work with each year is Endurox R4.

Chapter 20

AN EXERCISER'S DIET

A radical change in the foods you eat is not a good idea, and usually leads to problems. In this chapter, I will explain the items that are most important, and can help in maintaining good overall health and fitness. But, please, don't make radical diet changes.

As a regular exerciser you will not need a significant increase in vitamins and minerals, protein, etc. But if you don't get these ingredients for several days in a row, you will feel the effects when you try to exercise.

MOST IMPORTANT NUTRIENT: WATER

Whether you prefer water, juice or other fluids, drink regularly throughout the day. Under normal circumstances, your thirst is a good guide for fluid consumption. I will not tell you that you must drink 8 glasses of water a day, because I've not seen any research to back this up. Fluid researchers who follow this topic tell me that the research says that if we drink regularly and when thirsty, fluid levels are replaced fairly quickly.

If you have to take bathroom stops during walks or runs, you are probably drinking too much—either before or during the exercise. During an exercise session of 60 minutes or less, most exercisers don't need to drink at all. The intake of fluid before exercise should be arranged so that the excess fluid is eliminated before the run. Each person is a bit different, so you will have to find a routine that works for you. Most find that by drinking fluid 60 minutes or more before the start, the potty stop(s) can be made before running.

Even during extremely long runs of over 4 hours, medical experts from major marathons recommend no more than 27 oz of fluid an hour.

SWEAT THE ELECTROLYTES

Electrolytes are the salts that your body loses when you sweat: sodium, potassium, magnesium and calcium. When these minerals get too low, your fluid transfer system doesn't work as well and you may experience ineffective cooling, swelling of the hands, and other problems. Most runners have no problem replacing these in a normal diet, but if you are experiencing cramping during or after exercise, regularly, you may be low in sodium or potassium. The best product I've found for replacing these minerals is called SUCCEED. If you have high blood pressure (or any issue with electrolytes), get your doctor's guidance before taking any salt supplement.

Note: It is almost impossible to replace electrolytes with sports drinks during a run. The best time to "top off" electrolytes is the day before by drinking about 32 oz of a product like Accelerade throughout the day. Endurox R4 immediately after the long run has been shown to speed recovery.

PRACTICAL EATING ISSUES

- You don't need to eat before a run, unless your blood sugar is low.

- Reload most effectively by eating within 30 min of the finish of a run (80% carb/20% protein).

- Eating or drinking too much right before the start of a run will interfere with deep breathing, and may cause side pain. The food or fluid in your stomach limits your intake of air into the lower lungs, and restricts the action of the diaphragm.

- If your blood sugar is low at the end of your long runs, take some blood sugar booster with you (see the previous chapter for suggestions).

- It is never a good idea to eat a huge meal. Those who claim that they must "carbo load", with a large meal the night before, are rationalizing their desire to eat a lot of food. Eating a big meal the night before (or the day of) a long run can be a real problem. You will have a lot of food in your gut, and you will be bouncing up and down for an extended period. Get the picture?

When you are sweating a lot, it is a good idea to drink several glasses throughout the day of a good electrolyte beverage. Accelerade, by Pacific Health Labs, is the best I've seen for both maintaining fluid levels and electrolyte levels.

RUN-WALK EATING SCHEDULE

- 1 hour before a morning run: either a cup of coffee or a glass of water.

- 30 min before any run (if blood sugar is low): approx. 100 calories of Acclerade.

- Within 30 min after a run: approx. 200 calories of a 80% carb/20% protein (Endurox R4, for example).

- If you are sweating a lot during hot weather, 3-4 glasses of a good electrolyte beverage like Accelerade throughout the day—not during a run.

Hint: I carry with me little packets of coffee concentrate and can have a cup of coffee quickly. Caffeine, when taken about an hour before exercise, engages the systems that enhance running and extend endurance.

MEAL IDEAS

Breakfast options

1. Whole-grain bread made into French toast with fruit yogurt, juice, or frozen juice concentrate as syrup.

2. Whole-grain pancakes with fruit and yogurt.

3. A bowl of Grape Nuts Cereal, skim milk, non-fat yogurt, and fruit.

4. Smoothie with fiber, fruit, juice, yogurt, etc.

Lunch options

1. Tuna fish sandwich, whole-grain bread, a little low-fat mayo, cole slaw (with fat-free dressing).

2. Turkey breast sandwich with salad, low-fat cheese, celery and carrots.

3. Veggie burger on whole-grain bread, low-fat mayo, salad of choice.

4. Spinach salad with peanuts, sunflower seeds, almonds, low-fat cheese, non-fat dressing, whole-grain rolls or croutons.

Dinner options

There are lots of great recipes in publications such as **Cooking Light.** The basics are listed below. What makes the meal come alive are the seasonings which are listed in the recipes. You can use a variety of fat substitutes.

1. Fish or lean chicken breast or tofu (or other protein source) with whole-wheat pasta, and steamed vegetables.

2. Rice with vegetables, and a protein source.

3. Dinner salad with lots of different vegetables, nuts, lean cheese or turkey, or fish, or chicken.

I recommend Nancy Clark's books. Her **Sports Nutrition Guidebook** is a classic.

Chapter 21

STAYING MOTIVATED

- Consistency is the most important part of conditioning and fitness.
- Motivation is the most important factor in being consistent.
- You can gain control over your motivation—every day.

The choice is yours. You can take control over your attitude, or you can let yourself be swayed by outside factors that will leave you on a motivational roller coaster: fired up one day, with no desire the next. Getting motivated on a given day can sometimes be as simple as saying a few key words and taking a walk. But staying motivated usually requires a strategy or motivational training program. To understand the process, we must first look inside your head.

A DISCONNECTION BETWEEN THE LEFT BRAIN AND THE RIGHT BRAIN

The brain has two hemispheres that are separated and don't interconnect. The logical left brain conducts our business activities, trying to steer us into pleasure and away from discomfort. The creative and intuitive right side is an unlimited source of solutions to problems and connections to hidden strengths.

Stress activates the negative left brain. As we accumulate stress, the left brain sends us a stream of logical messages that tell us "slow down", "stop and you'll feel better", "this isn't your day" and even philosophical messages like "why are you doing this". We are all capable of staying on track, and maintaining motivation even when the left brain is saying these things.

Take control through mental drills. The first important step in taking command over motivation is to ignore the left brain unless there is a legitimate reason of health or safety (very rare). You can deal with the left brain, through a series of mental training drills. These drills allow the right side of the brain to work on solutions to the problems you are having. As the negative messages spew out of the left brain, the right brain doesn't argue. By using the information below, you can prepare for the challenges ahead, while empowering yourself to deal with the problems and to become mentally tough. But even more important, you will have three strategies for success.

DRILL #1 REHEARSING SUCCESS

GETTING OUT THE DOOR AFTER A HARD DAY

By rehearsing yourself through a motivation problem, you help yourself to become more consistent, which sets the stage for improvement. You must first have a goal that is doable, and a rehearsal situation that is realistic. Let's learn by doing:

1. State your desired outcome: To be walking and running from my house after a hard day.

2. Detail the challenges: Low blood sugar and fatigue, a stream of negative messages, need to get the evening meal ready to be cooked, overwhelming desire to feel relaxed.

3. Break up the challenge into a series of actions, which lead you through the mental barriers, no one of which is challenging to the left brain.

- You're driving home at the end of the day, knowing that it is your exercise day but you have no energy.

- Your left brain says: "You're too tired; take the day off. You don't have the energy to run-walk".

- So you say to the left brain: "I'm not going to exercise. I'll put on some comfortable shoes and clothes."

- Eat and drink, get food preparation going for dinner, and feel relaxed.

- You're in your room, putting on comfortable clothes and shoes (they just happen to be used for running-walking).

- You're drinking coffee (tea, diet cola, etc.) and eating a good tasting energy snack, as you get the food prepared to go into the oven.

- Stepping outside, you check on the weather.

- You're walking to the edge of your block to see what the neighbors are doing.

- As you cross the street, you're on your way.

- The endorphins are kicking in, you feel good, you want to continue.

4. Rehearse the situation over and over, fine-tuning it so that it becomes integrated into the way you think and act.

5. Finish by mentally enjoying the good feelings experienced with the desired outcome. You have felt the good attitude, the vitality, the glow from a good run-walk, and you are truly relaxed. So revisit these positive feelings at the end of each rehearsal.

GETTING OUT THE DOOR EARLY IN THE MORNING

The second most common motivational problem that I'm asked about relates to the comfort of the bed, when you awaken knowing that it is time for exercise.

1. State your desired outcome: To be walking and running away from the house early in the morning

2. Detail the challenges: Desire to lie in bed, no desire to exert yourself so early. The stress of the alarm clock, and having to think about what to do next when the brain isn't working very fast.

3. **Break up the challenge into a series of actions, which lead you through the mental barriers, not one of which is challenging to the left brain.**

  - The night before, lay out your running clothes and shoes, near your coffee pot, so that you don't have to think.

  - Set your alarm, and say to yourself over and over: "alarm off, feet on the floor, to the coffee pot" or...."alarm, floor, coffee". As you repeat this, you visualize doing each action without thinking. By repeating it, you lull yourself to sleep. You have also been programming yourself for action in the morning.

  - The alarm goes off. You shut it off, put feet on the floor, and head to the coffee pot—all without thinking.

  - You're putting on one piece of clothing at a time, sipping coffee, never thinking about exercise.

  - With coffee cup in hand, you walk out the door to see what the weather is like.

  - Sipping coffee, you walk to edge of your block or property to see what the neighbors are doing.

  - Putting coffee down, cross the street—you've made the break!

  - The endorphins are kicking in, you feel good, you want to continue.

Rehearsals become patterns of behavior more easily if you don't think but just move from one action to the next. The power of the rehearsal is that you have formatted your brain for a series of actions so that you don't have to think as you move from one action to the next. As you repeat the pattern, revising it for real life, you become what you want to be. You are successful!

DRILL #2 MAGIC WORDS

Even the most motivated person has sections during a tough exercise session when they want to quit. By using a successful brainwashing technique, you can pull yourself through these negative thoughts, and feel so good at the end. On these days you have not only reached the finish line—you've overcome challenges to get there. Here's how it works.

Each of us have characteristic problems that reoccur. These are the ones that we can also expect to bother us in the future. Go back in your memory bank and pull out instances when you started to lose motivation due to these, but finished and overcame the challenge.

Relax.......Power.......Glide

In really tough runs, I have three such challenges: 1) I become tense when I get really tired, worried that I will struggle badly at the end. 2) I feel the loss of the bounce and strength I had at the beginning, and worry that there will be no strength at the end. 3) My form starts to get ragged and I worry about further deterioration of muscles and tendons and more fatigue due to "wobbling".

Over the past three decades I have learned to counter these three problems with the magic words "Relax...Power....Glide". The visualization of each of these positives helps a little. The real magic comes from the association I have made with hundreds of situations when I started to "lose it" in one of the three areas, but overcame the problems. Each time I overcome one or more of the problems, I associate the experience with these magic words and add to the magic.

Now, when something starts to go wrong, I repeat the three words, over and over. Instead of increasing my anxiety, I get calm. Even though I don't feel as strong at 5 miles as I did in the first one, I'm empowered just by knowing that I can draw upon my past experience. And when my legs lose the efficient path and bounce, I make adjustments and keep going.

I believe that when I say magic words that are associated with successful experience, there are two positive effects. Saying the words floods the brain with positive memories. For a while, the negative messages of the left brain don't have a chance and you can get down the road a mile or two. But the second effect   may be more powerful. The words directly link you to the right brain, which works intuitively to make the same connections that allowed you solve the problems and get on to success that day.

To be successful, you only need to finish the walk-run. Most of the time you can get through the "bad parts" by not giving up, and simply put one foot in front of the other. As you push beyond the negative left brain messages you develop confidence to do this again, and again. Feel free to use my magic words, or develop your own.

DRILL # 3 DIRTY TRICKS

The strategy of the rehearsal drill will get you focused, organized, while reducing stress for the first few miles. Magic words will pull you along through most of the rest of the challenging sessions. But on the really rough days, it helps to have some dirty tricks to play on the left side of the brain.

These are quick fixes that distract the left brain for a while, allowing you to get down the road for a half mile or so. These imaginative and sometimes crazy images don't have to have any logic behind them. But when you counter a left brain message with a creative idea, you have a window of opportunity to get closer to the end of the run.

THE GIANT INVISIBLE RUBBER BAND

When I get tired on long or hard runs, I unpack this secret weapon, and throw it around someone ahead of me. For a while, the person doesn't realize that he or she has been "looped" and continues to push onward while I get the benefit of being pulled along. After a while of getting into this image, I have to laugh at myself for believing in such an absurd notion. But laughing activates the creative right side of the brain. This usually generates several more entertaining ideas, especially when you do this on a regular basis.

The right brain has millions of dirty tricks. Once you activate it, you're likely to experience its solutions to problems you are currently having. It can entertain you as you get another 400-800 yards closer to your finish.

For many more dirty tricks and mental strategies, see *Galloway's Book on Running* (3rd Edition) and *Marathon—You Can Do It.*

Chapter 22

CROSS-TRAINING: EXERCISE FOR THE NON-RUNNING DAYS

My run-walk method has helped tens of thousands of new runners avoid injury, and enjoy the increased vitality and attitude that comes with regular running. A growing percentage of these new runners have had such a good experience with running injury free that they think they are immune to aches and pains. They are wrong.

TOO MUCH OF A GOOD THING

When you run, you must lift your body weight off the ground, and then absorb the shock as it comes back down. If you are doing this every other day, the limited damage can almost always be repaired, and your fitness improved. Many runners—even in their 50s and 60s don't ever have lingering problems.

Once runners get into a regular running routine, and enjoy the vitality and attitude boost, some will try to sneak in an extra day or two on the days they should be resting the running muscles. The same people that had trouble getting motivated for months, suddenly get out of control, and suffer from aches and pains. The logic goes like this: if the minimal amount of running made them feel pretty good, increasing the mileage has to make them feel much better. The reality is that adding one or two extra running days doubles or triples the injury risk.

CROSS-TRAINING ACTIVITIES

The middle ground is to run one day, and cross train the next. Cross-training simply means "alternative exercise" to running. Your goal is to find exercises that give you the same type of boost as you receive from running, but without tiring the workhorses of running: calf muscles, achilles tendon, ankle, foot.

The other exercises may not deliver the same good feelings—but they can come close. Many runners like to use a combination of 3 or 4 different ones in a session. But even if you don't feel exactly the same way, you'll receive the relaxation that comes from exercise, while burning calories and fat.

WHEN YOU ARE STARTING TO DO ANY EXERCISE (OR STARTING AFTER A LAYOFF)

1. Start with 5 easy minutes of each exercise, rest for 20 or more minutes and do 5 more easy minutes.

2. You may do 3-5 different exercises during a cross-training session if they don't use the same muscles.

3. Take a day of rest after each type of exercise (you can do another exercise the next day).

4. Increase by 2-3 additional minutes on each exercise, each session until you accumulate the number of minutes that you feel comfortable doing.

5. Once you have reached two 15-minute sessions, you could shift to one 22- to 25-minute session and increase by 2-3 more minutes per session if you wish.

6. It's best to not exercise the day before a long run.

7. To maintain your conditioning in each exercise it's best to do one session a week of 10 minutes or more once your reach that amount.

8. The maximum cross-training is up to the individual. As long as you are feeling fine for the rest of the day and are having no trouble with your runs, the length of your cross-training is up to you.

WATER RUNNING CAN IMPROVE YOUR RUNNING FORM

All of us have little flips and side motions of our legs that interfere with our running efficiency. The resistance of the water, during a water running workout, forces your legs to find a more efficient path. In addition, several leg muscles are strengthened which can help to keep your legs on a smoother path when they get tired at the end of a long run.

HERE'S HOW!

You'll need a flotation belt for this exercise. The product "Aqua Jogger" is designed to float you off the bottom of the pool. Tighten the belt so that it's snug but does not feel too tight. There are many other devices to keep you floating, including simple ski float belts and life jackets.

Get in the deep end of the pool and move your legs through a running motion: little or no knee lift, kicking out slightly in front of you, and bringing the leg behind, with the foot coming up so that the lower and upper leg make a 90-degree angle behind you. As in running, your lower leg should be parallel with the horizon.

If you are not feeling much exertion, you're probably lifting the knees too high and moving your legs through a tiny range of motion. To get the benefit, an extended running motion is needed.

It's important to do water running once a week to keep the adaptations that you have gained. If you miss a week, you should reduce the length of your workout by a few minutes from your previous session. If you miss more than 3 weeks, start back at two 5- to 8-minute sessions.

FAT-BURNING AND OVERALL FITNESS EXERCISES

NORDIC TRACK

This exercise machine simulates the motion used in cross-country skiing. It is one of the better cross-training modes for fat burning because it allows you to use a large number of muscle cells while raising body temperature. If you exercise at an easy pace, you can get into the fat-burning zone (beyond 45 minutes) after a gradual buildup to that amount. This exercise requires no pounding of the legs or feet and (unless you push too hard or too long) allows you to run as usual the next day.

ROWING MACHINE

There are a number of different types of rowing machines. Some force the legs to work a bit too hard for runners, but most allow you to use a wide variety of lower and upper body muscle groups. If you have the right machine for you, it's possible to continue to exercise for about as long as you wish, once you have gradually worked up to this. Most of the better machines promote the use of a large number of muscle cells, raise the body temperature, and can be continued for more than three-quarters of an hour—so they're fat-burners.

CYCLING

Indoor cycling (on an exercise cycle) is a better fat-burning exercise than outdoor cycling, because it raises your body temperature a bit more. The muscles used in both indoor and outdoor cycling are mostly the quadriceps muscles—on the front of the upper thigh—reducing the total number of muscle cells in use compared with the two other modes above.

DON'T FORGET WALKING!

Walking can be done all day long, burning a significant number of calories each day. I call walking a "stealth fat-burner" exercise because it is so easy to walk mile after mile—especially in small doses. But it is also an excellent cross-training exercise—this includes walking on the treadmill.

CROSS-TRAINING FOR THE UPPER BODY

WEIGHT TRAINING

While weight work is not a great fat-burning exercise, and does not directly help you running, it can be done on non-running days, or on running days (after a run).

There are many different ways to build strength. If interested, find a coach that can help you build strength in the muscle groups you want to strengthen. As mentioned previously in this book, weight training for the legs is not recommended.

SWIMMING

While not a fat-burner, swimming strengthens the upper body, improving cardiovascular fitness and endurance in those muscles. Swimming can be done on both running days and non-running days.

DON'T DO THESE ON NON-RUNNING DAYS!

The following exercises will tire the muscles used for running and keep them from recovering between run days. If you really like to do any of these exercises, you can do them after a run, on a running day.

- Stair machines
- Stair aerobics
- Weight training for the leg muscles
- Power walking—especially on a hilly course
- Spinning classes (on a bicycle) in which you get out of your seat

Chapter 23

DEALING WITH THE WEATHER

"Neither rain, nor ice, nor heat, nor gloom, nor night shall keep us from our run"

Sometimes, on the snowy, rainy, brutally cold days, I yearn for the early days of running when we had an excuse for not braving the elements. Today, however, there are garments for each of the above, head to toe. Yes, technology has taken away most of our excuses for not exercising. But runners can be very creative. Every year I hear a few new excuses from those who rise to the occasion and find some reason why they can't exercise. In reality, even if you don't have the clothing for hot or cold weather, you can run/walk indoors—on treadmills, in malls or stadiums, or at a gym.

A few years ago, I ran a race in Fairbanks, Alaska. I had to ask the members of the local running club what was the lowest temperature anyone had endured. The winner had run a 10K in minus 66 (not wind-chill, this was the real thing: bulb temperature). He said that it really didn't feel that cold. The fact is that clothing designers have responded to the needs of runners during extreme weather conditions, making it possible to run, fairly comfortably, in sub-zero conditions. I will admit, however, that if it is minus 66, I can't run because I have to rearrange my running shoes next to a warm fire.

HOT WEATHER

I've heard rumors of an air-conditioned suit for the heat, but haven't seen it offered by the clothing manufacturers. I could have used this when I ran a marathon in Key West, FL, when it was 95 degrees for the last 20 miles of the race. After decades of running in hot weather areas, mostly in Florida and Georgia, with some time spent in Hawaii and the Philippines, I haven't seen much in clothing that lowers body temperature. The best you can hope for is to minimize the rise, while you feel cooler, and a bit more comfortable.

When you exercise strenuously in high heat (above 70°F), or moderate heat (above 60°F) with high humidity (above 50%) you raise core body temperature. Most beginning runners will see the internal temperature rise when the outside thermometer rises. This triggers a release of blood into the capillaries of your skin to help cool you down. But this diversion reduces the blood supply available to your exercising muscles, meaning that you will have less blood and less oxygen delivered to the power source that moves you forward—and less blood to move out the waste products from these work sites.

So the bad news is that in warm weather you are going to feel worse and run slower. If you build up the heat too quickly, stay out too long, or run too fast—for you—the result could be heat disease. Make sure that you read the section on this health problem at the end of this chapter. The good news is that you can adapt to these conditions to some extent, as you learn the best time of the day, clothing to wear, and other tricks to keep you cool. But there are some other good options below, so read on.

RUNNING THROUGH THE SUMMER HEAT

1. Run before the sun gets above the horizon. Get up early during warm weather and you will significantly reduce the dramatic stress increase due to sunlight. This is particularly a problem in humid areas. Early morning is usually the coolest time of the day, also. Without having to deal with the sun, most runners can gradually adapt to heat. At the very least, your runs will be more enjoyable. Note: be sure to take care of safety issues.

2. If you must run when the sun is up, pick a shady course. Shade provides significant relief in areas of low humidity, and some relief in humid environments.

3. Evening and night running is usually cooler in areas with low humidity. In humid environments there may not be much relief.

4. Have an indoor facility available. With treadmills, you can exercise in air conditioning. If a treadmill bores you, alternate segments of 5-10 minutes—one segment outdoor, and the next indoor.

5. Don't wear a hat! You lose most of your body heat through the top of your head. Covering the head will cause a quicker internal buildup of heat.

6. Wear light clothing, but not cotton. Many of the new, technical fibers (Polypro, Coolmax, Drifit, etc.) will move moisture away from your skin, producing a cooling effect. Cotton soaks up the sweat, making the garment heavier without providing much of a cooling effect.

7. Pour water over your head. Evaporation not only helps the cooling process—it makes you feel cooler. If you can bring along ice water with you, you will feel a lot cooler as you squirt some regularly over the top of your head.

8. Do your run-walks in installments. It is fine, on a hot day, to put in your 30 minutes by doing 10 in the morning, 10 at noon and 10 at night. The long run, however, should be done at one time.

9. Take a pool break, or a shower chill-down. During a run, it really helps to take a 2- to 4-minute dip in a pool or a shower. Some runners in hot areas run loops around their neighborhood and let the hose run over the head each lap. The pool is especially helpful in soaking out excess body temperature. I have run in 97-degree temperatures at our Florida retreat area, breaking up a 5-mile run into 3 x 1.7 mi. Between each, I take a 2- to 3-minute "soak break" and get back out there. It was only at the end of each segment that I felt hot again.

10. Sunscreen—be sure to protect yourself. Some products, however, produce a coating on the skin, slowing down the perspiration and causing an increase in body temperature buildup. Consult with a dermatologist for your specific needs—or find a product that doesn't block the pores.

11. Drink 6-8 oz of a sports drink like Accelerade or water, at least every 2 hours, or when thirsty, throughout the day during hot weather.

12. Look at the clothing thermometer at the end of this section. Wear loose fitting garments that have some texture in the fabric. Texture will limit or prevent the perspiration from causing a clinging and sticking to the skin.

13. If your only option is going outside on a very hot day, you have my permission to rearrange your running shoes—preferably in front of the air conditioning vent. Water running is a great option on hot days.

HOT WEATHER SLOW-DOWN

As the temperature rises above 55°F, your body starts to build up heat, but most runners aren't significantly slowed until 60°F. If you make the adjustments early, you won't have to suffer later and slow down a lot more at that time. The baseline for this table is 60°F or 14°C.

Between 60°F and 65°F	slow down 30 seconds/mile slower than you would run at 60°F
Between 14°C and 17°C	slow down 20 seconds/kilometer than you would run at 14°C
Between 66°F and 69°F	slow down one minute/mile slower than you would run at 60°F
Between 18°C and 19°C	slow down 40 seconds/kilometer slower than you would run at 14°C
Between 70°F and 75°F	slow down 1:30/mile slower than you would run at 60°F
Between 19°C and 22°C	slow down one minute/kilometer slower than you would run at 14°C
Between 76°F and 80°F	slow down 2 min/mile slower than you would run at 60°F
Between 23°C and 25°C	slow down 1:20/kilometer slower than you would run at 14°C
Above 80°F and 25°C	be careful, take extra precautions to avoid heat disease Or...exercise indoors Or...arrange your shoes next to the air conditioner

HEAT DISEASE ALERT!

While it is unlikely that you will push yourself into heat disease, the longer you are exercising in hot (and/or humid) conditions, the more you increase the likelihood of this dangerous medical situation. That's why I recommend breaking up your exercise into short segments when it's hot and you must run outdoors. Be sensitive to your reactions to the heat, and those of the runners around you. When one of the symptoms is present, this is normally not a major problem unless there is significant distress. But when several are experienced, take action because heat disease can lead to death. It's always better to be conservative: stop the workout and cool off.

SYMPTOMS

- Intense heat buildup in the head
- General overheating of the body
- Significant headache
- Significant nausea or vomiting
- General confusion and loss of concentration
- Loss of muscle control
- Excessive sweating and then cessation of sweating
- Clammy skin
- Excessively rapid breathing
- Muscle cramps
- Feeling faint
- Diarrhea

RISK FACTORS

- Viral or bacterial infection
- Taking medication—especially cold medicines, diuretics, medicines for diarrhea, antihistamines, atropine, scopolamine, tranquilizers
- Dehydration (especially due to alcohol)
- Severe sunburn
- Overweight
- Lack of heat training
- Exercising more than one is used to
- Occurrence of heat disease in the past
- Several nights of extreme sleep deprivation
- Certain medical conditions, including high cholesterol, high blood pressure, extreme stress, asthma, diabetes, epilepsy, drug use (including alcohol), cardiovascular disease, smoking, or a general lack of fitness

TAKE ACTION! CALL 911

Use your best judgment, but in most cases anyone who exhibits two or more of the symptoms should get into a cool environment, and receive medical attention immediately. An extremely effective cool-off method is to soak towels, sheets or clothing in cool or cold water, and wrap them around the individual. If ice is available, sprinkle some ice over the wet cloth.

HEAT ADAPTATION WORKOUT

If you regularly force yourself to deal with body heat buildup, your body will get better at dealing with it. As with all training components, it is important to do this regularly.

You should be sweating to some extent at the end of the workout, although the amount and the duration of perspiration is an individual issue. If the heat (and/or humidity) is particularly high, cut back on the duration of the workout.

Note: Read the section on heat disease and stop this workout if you sense that you are even beginning to become nauseous, lose concentration or mental awareness of your condition, etc.

- Done on a short running day once a week
- Use the run-walk ratio that works for you, going at a comfortable pace
- Warm up with a 5-min walk and take a 5-min walk warm down
- Temperature should be between 75°F and 85°F (22-27°C) for best results
- Stop at the first sign of nausea or significant heat stress
- When less than 70°F (19°C), you can put on additional layers of clothing to simulate a higher temperature.
- First session, run-walk for only 3-4 minutes in the heat
- Each successive session, add 2-3 minutes

TIP: MAINTAINING HEAT TOLERANCE DURING THE WINTER

By putting on additional layers of clothing so that you sweat within 3-4 minutes of your run-walk, you can keep much of your summer heat conditioning that took so much work to produce. Continue to run for a total of 5-12 minutes at an easy pace.

DEALING WITH THE COLD

While most of my runs have been in temperatures above 60°F, I've also run in -30. I prepared for this run extensively and put on about as many layers as I had in my suitcase. My winter running guide quickly evaluated my clothing and found me lacking. After another two layers I was ready to go.

The specific type of garments, especially the one next to your skin, is an individual issue. I'm not going to get into the specifics here because the technology changes quickly. In general, you want your first layer to be comfortable and not too thick. There are a number of fabrics today, mostly man-made, that hold a comfortable amount of body heat close to the skin to keep you warm but don't let you overheat. Most of these same fibers allow for moisture, such as perspiration and rain, to be moved away from the skin—even as you run and walk. Not only do the technical fibers add to your comfort in winter, it almost eliminates a chill due to having wet skin underneath.

RUNNING THROUGH THE CHILL OF WINTER

1. Expand your lunch hour if you want to run outdoors. Midday is usually the warmest time of the day, so you will probably have to plan to arrive at work early (pay bills, run errands, etc.). The midday sun can make your outdoor running much more comfortable—even when it is very cold.

2. If early morning is the only time you can run, bundle up. The "clothing thermometer" at the end of this section will help you to dress for the temperature without overdressing.

3. Run into the wind at the start, particularly when you are running out and turning around. If you run with the wind at your back for the first half of the run you'll tend to sweat. When you turn into a cold wind, you'll chill down dramatically.

4. Membership in a health club will give you an indoor venue and other exercise options. Using a treadmill lets you run away from the wind chill. I have worked with many runners who hate running on treadmills, but also hate running for more than 15 minutes in the cold. Their solution is to alternate segments of 7-15 minutes—one segment outdoor, and the next indoor. Count the transition as a walk break. Health clubs expand your exercise horizons, offering a variety of alternative exercise.

5. One of your exercise days could be a triathlon—your choice of three exercises. You can do exercises out of your home, or at a health club. See the sidebar on "winter triathlon" for more information.

6. Seek out a large indoor facility near your office or home. In Houston, runners use the tunnels below city streets. Many northern cities offer skyways and allow runners and walkers to use them when traffic allows it. Domes, malls and civic centers often allow winter runners and walkers at certain times.

7. Wear a hat! You lose most of your body heat through the top of your head. Covering the head will help you retain body heat and stay warm.

8. Cover your extremities from the wind chill you produce when you run and walk in the cold! Protect ears, and hands, nose and generally the front of the face. Make sure that you protect the feet with socks that are thick enough. And men, wear an extra pair of underwear.

9. Do your run-walk in installments. It is fine, on a really cold day, to put in your 30 minutes by doing 10 in the morning, 10 at noon and 10 at night. Long runs need to be run continuously.

10. Take a "warm-up" break. Before you head out into the cold, walk and run in place, indoors. During a run, when you get really cold on the outside, it really helps to take a 2-4 minute walk indoors. Some runners schedule their walk breaks to coincide with buildings that allow public walking.

11. Vaseline—be sure to protect yourself wherever there is exposed skin on very cold days. One area, for example, is the skin around the eyes not protected by a ski mask, etc.

12. When you are exercising during the winter, indoor or outdoor, you will be losing almost as much in sweat as in the warm months. You should still drink at least 4-6 oz of a sports drink like Accelerade or water, at least every 2 hours, or when thirsty, throughout the day. During a long run, the recommended fluid intake is between 14 and 27 oz an hour.

13. Another reminder: Look at the clothing thermometer at the end of this section and customize it for your situation.

WINTER TRIATHLON

Energize your winter workouts by doing three or more segments during your training. Here's how it works:

1.   Select one day a week for your triathlon. Choose three activities.

2.   Outdoor activities: run-walk, cross-country skiing, skating, snowshoeing, etc.

3.   Indoor health club activities: run-walk, swim, stair machine, exercycle, rowing machine, etc.

4.   Indoor activities at home: exercise machines, stairs, weights, sit-ups, rope skipping, running in place, aerobic video exercise.

5.   Alternate the activities for about 5-10 minutes at a time.

6.   If desired, keep a log of how much work you do on each machine, miles run, minutes for each activity, etc.

7.   Expand to a pentathlon (5 events), decathlon (10 events) or whatever.

8.   Combine indoor and outdoor activities if you wish; set up your "world record" list.

CLOTHING THERMOMETER

After years of working with people in various climates, here are my recommendations for the appropriate clothing based upon the temperature. As always, however, wear what works best for you. The general rule is to choose your garments by function first. And remember that the most important layer for comfort is the one next to your skin. Garments made out of fabric labeled Polypro, Coolmax, Drifit, etc., hold enough body heat close to you in winter, while releasing extra heat to keep you warm. In summer and winter, these fabrics move moisture away from the skin—cooling you in hot weather, and avoiding a chill in the winter.

Temperature	What to wear
14°C or 60°F and above	Tank top or singlet, and shorts
9 to 13°C or 50 to 59°F	T-shirt and shorts
5 to 8°C or 40 to 49°F	Long-sleeve lightweight shirt, shorts or tights (or nylon long pants), mittens and gloves
0 to 4°C or 30 to 39°F	Long-sleeve, medium-weight shirt, and another T-shirt, tights and shorts, socks or mittens or gloves and a hat over the ears
−4 to −1°C or 20-29°F	Medium-weight, long-sleeve shirt, another T-shirt, tights and shorts, sox, mittens or gloves, and a hat over the ears
−8 to −3°C or 10-19°F	Medium-weight, long-sleeve shirt, and medium-/heavy-weight shirt, tights and shorts, nylon wind suit, top and pants, socks, thick mittens and a hat over the ears
−12 to −7°C or 0-9°F	Two medium- or heavy-weight long-sleeve tops, thick tights, thick underwear (especially for men), medium to heavy warm-up suit, gloves and thick mittens, ski mask, a hat over the ears, and vaseline covering any exposed skin.
−18 to −11°C or −15°F	Two heavy-weight, long-sleeve tops, tights and thick tights, thick underwear (and supporter for men), thick warm-up suit (top and pants), mittens over gloves, thick ski mask and a hat over ears, vaseline covering any exposed skin, thicker socks on your feet and other foot protection, as needed.
−20 both °C & °F	Add layers as needed

WHAT NOT TO WEAR

1. A heavy coat in winter. If the layer is too thick, you'll heat up, sweat excessively, and cool too much when you take it off.

2. No shirt for men in summer. Fabric that holds some of the moisture will give you more of a cooling effect as you run and walk.

3. Too much sunscreen—it can interfere with sweating. But be sure to apply adequate amounts to protect against skin cancer.

4. Socks that are too thick in summer. Your feet swell and the pressure from the socks can increase the chance of a black toenail and blisters.

5. Lime green shirt with bright pink polka dots (unless you have a lot of confidence and/or can run fast).

Chapter 24

DESTROYING EXCUSES

All of us have days when we don't feel like running. On some of those days you probably need a day off, due to too much running or other physical activity. But usually this is not the case. The fact is that when we are under stress in life (and who isn't), the left brain will have dozens of great reasons why we shouldn't run. They are all perfectly logical and accurate.

Each of us can choose whether to listen to the excuse or not. Once you quickly decide whether there is a medical (or other legitimate reason) why you shouldn't run, most of the time you'll conclude that the left brain is just trying to make you lazy.

Thinking ahead will not take any significant time away from your day, and will destroy most of these excuses. You'll discover pockets of time, more energy, quality time with kids, and more enjoyment from exercise than you thought possible.

The following is a list of excuses that most of us hear on a regular basis. With each, I've given a strategy for breaking through the excuse. Most of the time, it is as simple as just getting out the door and getting your feet moving. But overall, you are the captain of your ship. If you take charge over your schedule and your attitude, you will plan ahead. As you learn to ignore the left brain, and put one foot in front of the other, the endorphins start flowing, and the excuses start to melt away. Life is good!

"I don't have time to run"

Most of the recent US presidents have been runners, as well as most of their vice presidents. Are you busier than the president? There are always pockets of time, 5 minutes here, 10 minutes there, when you can insert a walk-run. With planning, you'll find several half-hours each day. Many runners find that as they get in better shape, they don't need as much sleep, which allows for a chunk of time before the day gets started. It all gets down to the question, "Are you going to take control over the organization of your day or not?" Once you look at your schedule, you'll usually discover other time blocks that allow you to do other things. By making time for a run, you will also tend to be more productive and efficient, more than "paying back" the time you spend running. Bottom line is that you have the time—take it and you will have more quality in your life.

"The run will hurt or make me tired"

Aches, pains, and lingering fatigue are produced by YOU. By slowing the pace and inserting more walk breaks, you can eliminate the potential negative effects of most runs. If you have a bad habit of pushing the pace too much in the beginning, then get control over yourself! Walk more in the beginning, and slow down your running pace. As you learn to slow down, you'll avoid pain and come away from the run with more energy.

"I need to spend some time with my kids"

There are a number of running strollers that allow parents to run with their kids. My wife and I logged thousands of miles with our first child in a single "baby jogger". We got a twin carrier after our second was born. With the right pacing, you can talk to the kids about anything, and they can't run or crawl away. Sorry, they don't have a model for teenagers.

Because we were with the kid(s) in close company, we found that we talked more, and got more feedback than doing other activities together. By bringing them along with you on a run, you become a great role model: even though busy, you take time to exercise and spend time with kids.

"I've got too much work to do"

There will always be work to do. Several surveys have found that runners get more work done on days they run. Running produces more energy and a better attitude, and reduces stress. Hundreds of runners have told me that the early morning run allowed the time and generated the mental energy to organize their day better than any other activity. Others said that the after-work run relieved stress and tied up the mental loose ends from the office. Clearly you will get as much (probably more) work done each day if you run regularly. It is up to you to take charge so that you will insert the run into your day.

"I don't have the energy to run today"

This is one of the easier ones to dissolve. Most of the runners who've worked with me, and had this excuse, had not been eating enough times a day. I don't mean eating more food. In most cases, the quantity of food is reduced.

However, by eating about every 2-3 hours, most people feel more energized, more of the time. Even if you aren't eating well during the day, you can overcome low blood sugar by having a "booster" snack about an hour before a run. Caffeine helps (as long as you don't have caffeine sensitivities). My dynamic food duo is an energy bar and a cup of coffee. Just carry some food with you and energize yourself before a run. On trips, I carry packets of Javette coffee concentrate so that I can have a cup of coffee almost anywhere.

"I don't have my running shoes and clothes with me"

Take an old bag (backpack, etc.) and load it with a pair of running shoes, a top for both winter and summer, shorts and warm-up pants, towel, deodorant, and anything else you would need for a run and clean-up. Put the bag next to the front door, or in the trunk of your car. Then, the next time you are waiting to pick up your child from soccer, you can do a quick change in the restroom and make some loops around the field.

"I'd rather be sitting on a couch eating candy"

Ok, now it's time for your "test". What is your response to this type of message?

Chapter 25

TROUBLESHOOTING

HOW DO I START BACK, WHEN I'VE HAD TIME OFF?

The longer you've been away from running, the slower you must return. I want to warn you now that you will reach a point when you feel totally back in shape—but you are not. Stay with the plan below for your return and when in doubt, be more conservative. Remember that you are in this for the long run!

Less than 2 weeks off— You will feel like you are starting over again, but should come back quickly. Let's say that you were at week 20, but had to take 10 days off. Start back at week 2 for the first week. If all is well, skip to weeks 3 or 4 for the second week. If that works well, gradually transition back to the schedule you were using before you had your layoff, over the next 2-3 weeks.

14 days to 29 days off— You will also feel like you are starting over again, and it will take longer to get it all back. Within about 5-6 weeks you should be back to normal. Use the schedule of your choice (from week 1) for two weeks. If there are no aches, pains or lingering fatigue, then use the schedule but skip every other week. After the fifth week, transition back into what you were doing before the layoff.

One month or more off— If you have not run for a month or more, start over again, like a beginner. Use the 'to finish' schedule in this book, following it exactly (from week 1) for the first few weeks. After 2-3 weeks, the safest plan is to continue with the schedule. But if you're having no aches and pains, and no lingering fatigue, you could increase more rapidly by skipping one week out of three. After 2 months of no problems, your conditioning will have returned.

IT HURTS! IS IT JUST A PASSING ACHE, OR A REAL INJURY?

Most of the aches and pains you feel when running will go away within a minute or two. If the pain comes on when running, just walk for an additional 2 minutes, jog a few strides, and walk another 2 minutes. If the pain comes back after doing this 4 or 5 times, stop running and walk. If the pain goes away when you walk, just walk for the rest of the workout.

Walking pain— When the pain stays around when walking, try a very short stride. Walk for a 30-60 seconds. If it still hurts when walking, try sitting down, and massaging the area that hurts, if you can. Sit for 2-4 minutes. When you try again to walk, and it still hurts, call it a day—your workout is over.

IT'S AN INJURY IF....

- There's inflammation—swelling in the area
- There's loss of function—the foot, knee, etc. doesn't work correctly
- There's pain—it hurts and keeps hurting or gets worse

TREATMENT SUGGESTIONS:

1. See a doctor who has treated other runners very successfully and wants to get you back on the road or trail.

2. Take at least 2-5 days off from any activity that could irritate it to get the healing started, more if needed.

3. If the area is next to the skin (tendon, foot, etc), rub a chunk of ice on the area(s)—constantly rubbing for 15 min until the area gets numb. Continue to do this for a week after you feel no symptoms. Ice bags and gel ice do no good at all in most cases.

4. If the problem is inside a joint or muscle, call your doctor and ask if you can use prescription strength anti-inflammatory medication. Don't take any medication without a doctor's advice—and follow that advice.

5. If you have a muscle injury, see a veteran sports massage therapist. Try to find one who has a lot of successful experience treating the area where you are injured. The magic fingers and hands can often work wonders.

This is advice from one runner to another. For more info on injuries, treatment, etc. see a doctor and read the "injury free" chapter in this book, and *Galloway's Book On Running* (3rd Edition).

NO ENERGY TODAY

There will be a number of days each year when you will not feel like exercising. On most of these, you can turn it around and feel great. Occasionally, you will not be able to do this, because of an infection, lingering fatigue, or other physical problems. Here's a list of things that can give you energy. If these actions don't lead you to a run, then read the nutrition sections—particularly the blood sugar section in this book—or in *Galloway's Book On Running* (3rd Edition).

1. Eat an energy bar, with water or caffeinated beverage, about an hour before the run. Caffeine helps!

2. Instead of #1, half an hour before exercising you could drink 100-200 calories of a sports drink that has a mix of 80% simple carbohydrate and 20% protein. The product Accelerade already has this ratio.

3. Just walk for 5 minutes away from your house, office, etc., and the energy often kicks in. Forward movement gets the attitude moving, too.

4. One of the prime reasons for no energy is that you didn't re-load within 30 minutes after your last exercise session: 200-300 calories of a mix that is 80% simple carbohydrate and 20% protein (Endurox R4 is the product that has this formulation).

5. Low-carb diets will result in low energy to get motivated before a workout, and often no energy to finish the workout.

6. In most cases it is fine to keep going even if you aren't energetic. But if you sense an infection, see a doctor. If the low energy stays around for several days, see a nutritionist that knows about the special needs of exercisers and/or get some blood work done. Lingering fatigue may be due to inadequate iron, B vitamins, energy stores, etc.

Note: If you have any problems with caffeine, don't consume any products containing it. As always, if you sense any health problem, see a doctor.

SIDE PAIN

This is very common, and usually has a simple fix. Normally it is not anything to worry about...it just hurts. This condition is due to 1) the lack of deep breathing, and 2) going a little too fast from the beginning of the run. You can correct #2 easily by walking more at the beginning, and slowing down your running pace.

Deep breathing from the beginning of a run can prevent side pain. This way of inhaling air is performed by diverting the air you breathe into your lower lungs. Also called "belly breathing", this is how we breathe when asleep, and it provides maximum opportunity for oxygen absorption. If you don't deep breathe when you run, and you are not getting the oxygen you need, the side pain will tell you. By slowing down, walking, and breathing deeply for a while, the pain may go away.

But sometimes it does not. Most runners just continue to run and walk with the side pain. In 50 years of running and helping others run, I've not seen any lasting negative effect from those who run with this type of side pain.

Tip: Some runners have found that side pain goes away if they tightly grasp a rock in the hand that is on the side of the pain. Squeeze it for 15 seconds or so. Keep squeezing 3-5 times.

You don't have to take in a maximum breath to perform this technique. Simply breathe a normal breath but send it to the lower lungs. You know that you have done this if your stomach goes up and down as you inhale and exhale. If your chest goes up and down, you are breathing shallowly.

Note: Never breathe in and out rapidly. This can lead to hyperventilation, dizziness, and fainting.

I FEEL GREAT ONE DAY...AND NOT THE NEXT

If you can solve this problem, you could become a very wealthy person. There are a few common reasons for this, but there will always be "those days" when the body doesn't seem to work right—the gravity seems heavier than normal—and you cannot find a reason.

1. Pushing through. In most cases, this is a one-day occurrence. Most runners just put more walking into the mix, and get through it. Before pushing, however, make sure that you don't have a medical reason why you feel bad. Don't exercise when you have a lung infection, for example.

2. Heat and/or humidity will make you feel worse. You will often feel great when the temperature is below 60°F and miserable when 80°F or above (especially at the end of the workout).

3. Low blood sugar can make any run a bad run. You may feel good at the start and suddenly feel like you have no energy. Every step seems to take a major effort. Read the chapter in this book about this topic.

4. Low motivation. Use the rehearsal techniques in the "staying motivated" chapter to get you out the door on a bad day. These have helped numerous runners turn their minds around—even in the middle of a run.

5. Infection can leave you feeling lethargic, achy, and unable to run at the same pace that was easy a few days earlier. Check the normal signs (fever, chills, swollen lymph glands, etc.) and at least call your doctor if you suspect something.

6. Medication and alcohol, even when taken the day before, can leave a hangover that dampens a workout.

7. Taking walk breaks more frequently and slowing the beginning pace can make the difference between a good day and a bad day. When your body is on the edge of fatigue or other stress, it only takes a few seconds too fast per mile, walking and/or running, to push into discomfort or worse.

CRAMPS IN THE MUSCLES

At some point, most people who run experience cramps. These muscle contractions usually occur in the feet or the calf muscles and may come during a run or walk, or they may hit at random. Most commonly, they will occur at night, or when you are sitting around at your desk or watching TV in the afternoon or evening.

Cramps vary in severity. Most are mild but some can grab so hard that they shut down the muscles and hurt when they seize up. Massage, and a short and gentle movement of the muscle can help to bring most of the cramps around. Odds are that stretching will make the cramp worse, or tear the muscle fibers.

Most cramps are due to overuse—exercising farther or faster than in the recent past, or continuing to put yourself at your limit, especially in warm weather. Look at the pace and distance of your runs and walks in your training journal to see if you have been running too far, or too fast, or both.

- Continuous running increases cramping. Taking walk breaks more often can reduce or eliminate cramps. Many runners who used to cramp when they ran a minute and walked a minute, stopped cramping with a ratio of run 30 seconds and walk 30-60 seconds.

- During hot weather, a good electrolyte beverage can help to replace the salts that your body loses in sweating. A drink like Accelerade, for example, can help to top off these minerals when you drink approx. 6-8 oz every 1-2 hours throughout the day.

- On very long hikes, walks or runs, however, the continuous sweating, especially when drinking a lot of fluid, can push your sodium levels too low and produce muscle cramping. If this happens regularly, a buffered salt tablet has helped greatly: Succeed.

- Many medications, especially those designed to lower cholesterol, have as one of their known side effects, muscle cramps. Runners who use medications and cramp should ask their doctor if there are alternatives.

HERE ARE SEVERAL WAYS OF DEALING WITH CRAMPS:

1. Take a longer and more gentle warm-up.

2. Shorten your run segment.

3. Slow down your walk, and walk more.

4. Shorten your distance on a hot/humid day.

5. Break your run up into two segments.

6. Look at any other exercise that could be causing the cramps.

7. Take a buffered salt tablet at the beginning of your exercise.

8. Shorten your stride—especially on hills.

Note: If you have high blood pressure, ask your doctor before taking any salt product.

UPSET STOMACH OR DIARRHEA

Sooner or later, virtually every runner has at least one episode with nausea or diarrhea (N/D). It comes from the buildup of total stress that you accumulate. Most commonly, it is the stress of running on that day due to the causes listed below. But stress can come from many unique conditions within the individual. Your body triggers the N/D to get you to reduce the exercise, which will reduce the stress. Here are the common causes.

1. Running too fast or too far is the most common cause. Runners are confused about this, because the pace doesn't feel too fast in the beginning. Each person has a level of fatigue that triggers these conditions. Slowing down and taking more walk breaks will help you manage the problem.

2. Eating too much or too soon before the run. Your system has to work hard when you're running, and works hard to digest food. Doing both at the same time raises stress and results in nausea, etc. Having food in your stomach in the process of being digested is an extra stress and a likely target for elimination.

3. Eating a diet high in fat or protein. Even one meal that has over 50% of the calories in fat or protein can lead to N/D hours later.

4. Eating too much the afternoon or evening on the day before. A big evening meal will still be in the gut the next morning. When you bounce up and down on a run, which you will, you add stress to the system often producing (N/D).

5. Heat and humidity are a major cause of these problems. Some people don't adapt to heat well and experience N/D with minimal buildup of temperature or humidity. But in hot conditions, everyone has a core body temperature increase that will result in significant stress to the system—often causing nausea, and sometimes diarrhea. By slowing down, taking more walk breaks, and pouring water over your head, you can manage this better. The best time to exercise in warm weather is before the sun gets above the horizon.

6. Drinking too much water before a run. If you have too much water in your stomach, and you are bouncing around, you put stress on the digestive system. Reduce your intake to the bare minimum. Most runners don't need to drink any fluid before a run that is 60 minutes or less.

7. Drinking too much of a sugar/electrolyte drink. Water is the easiest substance for the body to process. The addition of sugar and/or electrolyte minerals, as in a sports drink, makes the substance harder to digest for many runners. During a run (especially on a hot day) it is best to drink only water.

8. Drinking too much fluid too soon after a run. Even if you are very thirsty, don't gulp down large quantities of any fluid. Try to drink no more than 6-8 oz, every 20 minutes or so. If you are particularly prone to this N/D, just take 2-4 sips, every 5 minutes or so. When the body is very stressed and tired, it's not a good idea to consume a sugar drink. The extra stress of digesting the sugar can lead to problems.

9. Don't let running be stressful to you. Some runners get too obsessed about getting their run in or running at a specific pace. This adds stress to your life. Relax and let your run diffuse some of the other tensions in your life.

HEADACHE

There are several reasons why runners get headaches on runs. While uncommon, they happen to the average runner about 1-5 times a year. The extra stress that running puts on the body can trigger a headache on a tough day—even considering the relaxation that comes from the run. Many runners find that a dose of an over-the-counter headache medication takes care of the problem. As always, consult with your doctor about use of medication. Here are the causes/solutions.

Dehydration—if you run in the morning, make sure that you hydrate well the day before. Avoid alcohol if you run in the mornings and have headaches. Also watch the salt in your dinner meal the night before. A good sports drink like Accelerade, taken throughout the day the day before, will help to maintain your fluid levels and your electrolytes. If you run in the afternoon, follow the same advice leading up to your run on the day of the run.

Medications can often produce dehydration headaches—there are some medications that make runners more prone to headaches. Check with your doctor.

Too hot for you—run at a cooler time of the day (usually in the morning before the sun gets above the horizon). When on a hot run, pour water over your head.

Running a little too fast—start all runs more slowly, walk more during the first half of the run.

Running farther than you have run in the recent past—monitor your mileage and don't increase more than about 15% farther than you have run on any single run in the past week.

Low blood sugar level—be sure that you boost your BLS with a snack, about 30-60 min before you run. If you are used to having it, caffeine in a beverage can sometimes help this situation also.

If prone to migraines—generally avoid caffeine, and try your best to avoid dehydration. Talk to your doctor about other possibilities.

Watch your neck and lower back—if you have a slight forward lean as you run, you can put pressure on the spine—particularly in the neck and lower back. Read the form chapter in this book and run upright.

SHOULD I RUN WHEN I HAVE A COLD?

There are so many individual health issues associated with a cold that you must talk with a doctor before exercising when you have an infection. Usually you will be given the OK to gently exercise. Check with the doctor.

Lung infection—don't run! A virus in the lungs can move into the heart and kill you. Lung infections are usually indicated by coughing.

Common cold? there are many infections that initially seem to be a normal cold but are not. At least call your doctor's office to get clearance before running. Be sure to explain how much you are running, and what, if any medication you are taking.

Throat infection and above—most runners will be given the OK, but check with the doc.

STREET SAFETY

Each year several runners are hit by cars when running. Most of these accidents are preventable. Here are the primary reasons and what you can do about them.

1. **The driver is intoxicated or preoccupied by cellphone, etc. Always be on guard— even when running on the sidewalk or pedestrian trail. Many of the fatal crashes occurred when the driver lost control of the car, and came up behind the runner, on the wrong side of the road. I know it is wonderful to be on "cruise control" in your right brain, but you can avoid a life-threatening situation if you will just keep looking around, and anticipate.**

2. **The runner dashes across an intersection against the traffic light. When running or walking with another person, don't try to follow blindly across an intersection. Runners who quickly sprint across the street without looking are often surprised by cars coming from unexpected directions. The best rule is the one that you heard as a child: When you get to an intersection, stop, see what the traffic situation is. Look both ways, and look both ways again (and again) before crossing. Have an option to bail out of the crossing if a car surprises you from any direction.**

3. Sometimes, runners wander out into the street as they talk and run. One of the very positive aspects of running becomes a negative one, in this case. Yes, chat and enjoy time with your friends. But every runner in a group needs to be responsible for his or her own safety, footing, etc. The biggest mistake I see is that the runners at the back of a group assume that they don't have to be concerned about traffic at all. This lack of concern makes for a very risky situation.

- In general, be ready to save yourself from a variety of traffic problems by following the rules below and any others that apply to specific situations. Even though the rules below seem obvious, many runners get hit by cars each year by ignoring them.

- Be constantly aware of vehicular traffic at all times.

- Assume that all drivers are drunk or crazy, or both. When you see a strange movement by a car, be ready to get out of the way.

- Mentally practice running for safety. Get into the practice of thinking ahead at all times, with a plan for that current stretch of road.

- Run as far off the road as you can. If possible run on a sidewalk or pedestrian trail.

- Run facing traffic. A high percentage of traffic deaths come from those who run with the flow of traffic, and do not see the threat from behind.

- Wear reflective gear at night. I've heard the accounts and this apparel has saved lives.

- Take control over your safety—you are the only one on the road who will usually save yourself.

DOGS

When you enter a dog's territory, you may be in for a confrontation. Here are my suggestions for dealing with your "dog days":

1. There are several good devices that will deter dogs: an old-fashioned stick, rocks, some electronic signal devices, and pepper spray. If you are in a new area, or an area of known dogs, I recommend that you have one of these at all times

2. At the first sign of a dog ahead, or barking, try to figure out where the dog is located, whether the dog is a real threat, and what territory the dog is guarding.

3. The best option is to run a different route.

4. If you really want or need to run past the dog, pick up a rock if you don't have another anti-dog device.

5. Watch the tail. If the tail does not wag, beware.

6. As you approach the dog it is natural for the dog to bark and head toward you. Raise your rock as if you will throw it at the dog. In my experience, the dog withdraws about 90% of the time. You may need to do this several times before getting through the dog's territory. Keep your arms up.

7. In a few cases you will need to throw the rock, and sometimes another if the dog keeps coming.

8. In less that 1% of the hundreds of dog confrontations I've had, there is something wrong with the dog, and it continues to move toward you. Usually the hair will be up on the dog's back. Try to find a barrier to get behind, yell loudly in hopes that the owner or someone will help you. If a car comes by, try to flag down the driver, and either stay behind the car as you get out of the dog's territory, or get in the car for protection if that is appropriate.

9. Develop your own voice. Some use a deep commanding voice, some use a high pitched voice. Whichever you use, exude confidence and command.

Chapter 26

TROUBLESHOOTING ACHES AND PAINS

At the first sign of soreness or irritation in the following areas, read the injury chapter. It is always better to take 2-3 days off from running, and then start back making some form adjustments and inserting more walk breaks. In most of these "pain sites," I've found that stretching aggravates the problem. For more information, see *Galloway's Book On Running* (3rd Edition).

SORENESS OR PAIN IN THE FRONT OF THE SHIN (ANTERIOR TIBIAL AREA)

Note: Even after you make the corrections, shin problems often take several weeks to heal. As long as the shin problem is not a stress fracture, easy running can often allow it to heal as quickly (or more quickly) than complete layoff. In general, most runners can run when they have shin splints—they just need to stay below the threshold of further irritation.

CAUSES:

1. Increasing too rapidly—just walk for 1-2 weeks, and walk with a short stride, gently.

2. Running too fast, even on one day—when in doubt, run slower and walk slower on all runs.

3. Running or walking with a stride that is too long—shorten stride and use more of a "shuffle".

SORENESS OR PAIN AT THE INSIDE OF THE LOWER LEG (POSTERIOR TIBIAL AREA)

CAUSES:

1. Same three causes as in anterior tibial shin splints, above.

2. More common with runners who overpronate. This means that they tend to roll to the inside of the foot as they push off.

3. Shoes may be too soft, allowing a floppy/pronated foot to roll inward more than usual.

CORRECTIONS:

1. Reduce stride length.

2. Slow the pace at the beginning and insert more walking into your run-walk ratio from the beginning.

3. If you are an overpronator on the forward part of your feet, get a stable, motion control shoe.

4. Ask your foot doctor if there is a foot device that can help you.

SHOULDER AND NECK MUSCLES TIRED AND TIGHT

PRIMARY CAUSE:
Leaning too far forward as you run.

OTHER CAUSES:

1. Holding arms too far away from the body as you run.

2. Swinging arms and shoulders too much as you run.

CORRECTIONS:

1. Use the "puppet on a string" image (detailed in the running form chapter) about every 4-5 minutes during all runs and walks—particularly the longer ones. This is noted in the section on posture.

2. Watch how you are holding your arms. Try to keep the arms close to the body.

3. Minimize the swing of your arms. Keep the hands close to the body, lightly touching your shirt or the outside of your shorts as your arms swing.

LOWER BACK: TIGHT, SORE, OR PAINFUL AFTER A RUN

CAUSES:

1. Leaning too far forward as you run.

2. Having a stride length that is too long for you.

CORRECTIONS:

1. Use the "puppet on a string" image several times on all runs and walks—particularly the longer ones. This is noted in the chapter on running form, in the section on posture.

2. Ask a physical therapist whether some strengthening exercise can help.

3. When in doubt, shorten your stride length.

4. For more information, see *Galloway's Book On Running* (3rd Edition).

KNEE PAIN AT THE END OF A RUN

CAUSES:

1. Stride length could be too long.

2. Doing too much, too soon.

3. Not inserting enough walk breaks, regularly, from the beginning.

4. When the main running muscles get tired, you will tend to wobble from side to side.

CORRECTIONS:

1. Shorten stride.

2. Stay closer to the ground, using more of a shuffle.

3. Monitor your mileage in a log book, and hold your increase to less than 10% a week.

4. Use more walk breaks during your run.

5. Start at a slower pace.

BEHIND THE KNEE: PAIN, TIGHTNESS, OR CONTINUED SORENESS OR WEAKNESS

CAUSES:

1. Stretching.

2. Overstriding—particularly at the end of the run.

CORRECTIONS:

1. Don't stretch.

2. Keep your stride length under control.

3. Keep feet low to the ground.

4. Hamstrings: Tightness, soreness, or pain

HAMSTRINGS: TIGHTNESS, SORENESS, OR PAIN

CAUSES:

1. Stretching.

2. Stride length too long.

3. Lifting the foot too high behind, as your leg swings back.

CORRECTIONS:

1. Don't stretch.

2. Maintain a short stride, keeping the hamstring relaxed—especially at the end of the run.

3. Take more walk breaks early in the run, possibly throughout the run.

4. As the leg swings behind you, let the lower leg rise no higher than a position that is parallel to the horizontal before swinging forward again.

5. Deep tissue massage can sometimes help with this muscle group.

QUADRICEPS (FRONT OF THE THIGH): SORE, TIRED, PAINFUL

CAUSES:
1. Lifting your knee too high—especially when tired.

2. Using the quads to slow down going downhill—because you were running too fast.

CORRECTIONS:
1. Maintain little or no knee lift—especially at the end of your run.

2. Run with a shuffle.

3. Let your stride get very short at the top of hills, and when tired—don't lengthen it.

4. If you are running too fast going down hills, keep shortening stride until you slow down, and/or take more walk breaks on the downhill.

SORE FEET OR LOWER LEGS

CAUSES:
1. Too much bounce.

2. Pushing off too hard.

3. Shoes don't fit correctly or are too worn out.

4. Insole of shoe is worn out.

CORRECTIONS:
1. Keep feet low to the ground.

2. Maintain a light touch of the feet.

3. Get a shoe check to see if your shoes are too worn.

4. You may need only a new insole.

Chapter 27

RUNNING AFTER 40, 50, 60, 70

Every year I hear dozens of people tell me they wish they could run, but they didn't start doing it when they were younger, and felt it was too late for them. Within a few minutes, these folks wish they hadn't said what they said to me. I tell them I work with hundreds of people every year who are in their 40s, 50s, 60s, 70s, and even 80s who are taking their first steps. Most of these folks become runners within 6 months. Many of them finish marathons—yes, even the 80-year-olds—within a year.

The principles of training which are described in this book apply to everyone—at any age. If you add a little stress followed by rest for recovery, your body rebuilds stronger.

The psychological rewards are the same at any age. Endorphins make your muscles feel better. You have a better attitude all day after a run. Each run brings a special relaxation not bestowed by other activities.